The Sunflower

The Sunflower

by Simon Wiesenthal
with a Symposium

SCHOCKEN BOOKS • NEW YORK

Mr. Wiesenthal's text and all contributions for the
Symposium received in German were translated by H.A.
Pichler. Contributions for the Symposium received in French
were translated by Mrs. Carol Pimental Pinto.

Library of Congress Cataloging in Publication Data

Wiesenthal, Simon.
    The sunflower.

    Translation of Die Sonnenblume.
    1. World War, 1939–1945—Personal
    narratives, Jewish. 2. Wiesenthal, Simon.
    Die Sonnenblume. I. Title.
D810.J4W5313 1976   179.7   75-35446

ISBN 0-8052-0-578-0

Manufactured in the United States of America
                    B 9 8 7

Contents

The Sunflower

Foreword by
Rabbi Barry Dov Schwartz

Before the war, Simon Wiesenthal was a successful architect in Lemberg, Galicia. He had graduated from the universities of Prague and Lemberg, and was awarded two engineering degrees. Until 1943, he practiced his profession in relative safety, but in October of that year he was arrested. Expecting the Gestapo to torture him, Wiesenthal tried to commit suicide. Following that attempt, he was shuttled across Europe from Poland to Austria through more than a dozen concentration camps, narrowly escaping death on numerous occasions. He finally reached the Mauthausen camp in February 1945; in May he was liberated by advancing American troops.

Eighty-nine of Wiesenthal's own relatives died at the hands of the Nazis. He had looked on helplessly as his mother was crammed into a freight car with hundreds of other elderly Jewish women; she died in the Belzec camp. His wife's mother was shot to death on the stairway of her home.

Since his release in 1945, Simon Wiesenthal has devoted his life to hunting down and bringing to trial the wartime criminals who in their tenacious fanaticism introduced to civilization the concept of systematic genocide. Wiesenthal's Jewish Documentation Center is located in Vienna, where thousands of former Nazis reside, many of them now government employees and police officials. Operating in a city sensitive to the implications of dishonor, Wiesenthal must be extremely cautious.

His methods of investigation are necessarily obscure, but since the liberation and the Dachau war trials he has been gathering and assimilating data and documents. In Europe, South America, and North America for thirty years Wiesenthal has been preparing dossiers, amassing files, taking anonymous leads from informants.

Wiesenthal's present activities include the publication of an Information Bulletin, in which he describes his latest activities and lists the names, aliases, and whereabouts of Nazis he has located, and the "tips" he has received about other wanted criminals. He is continuously procuring official documents regarding deportation methods and gassing procedures.

In the local Jewish Viennese newspaper, *Der Ausweg,* Wiesenthal shares unclassified material with his readers. In one of the issues, for example, he published a hazy photograph of an SS guard posing at Buchenwald with three men hanging from a tree behind him. Under the picture the caption reads: "Anyone who can identify the man in this photograph please contact the Documentation Center immediately."

Besides pursuing criminals, Wiesenthal also seeks witnesses. "Discovering witnesses is just as important as catching criminals," he has written. If no real witness can be produced, many times a Nazi can be set free. Witnesses have come from all over the world to identify Nazi tormentors.

Immediately after the war there was no dearth of pronouncements from world leaders of their dedication to punishing Nazis. Declarations were made, promises offered, and editorials written, but Time has proven the great Healer. "Bad times" are too embarrassing to be remembered. So Wiesenthal and the Jews must remember, for, as Wiesenthal wrote in *The New York Times*, "the schools would fail through their silence, the Church through its forgiveness, and the home through the denial and silence of the parents. The new generation has to hear what the older generation refuses to tell it." *The Sunflower* is remarkable and singular. It is not a history, not an autobiography, not a novel, nor a sermon, although perhaps a little of each. *The Sunflower* is a question. It leaves us precisely where the fate of European Jewry must leave us: in a state of quandary, of bewildered uncertainty. Why? How? The value of this brief volume is not in the story it tells, but in what it doesn't tell, what it relegates to the conscience of the reader. Ironically enough, it is Simon Wiesenthal who, by engaging in the apprehension of the guilty, serves as a sunflower to those who perished in torment. He and others like him are seeking justice—not revenge—for those who inflicted the worst crimes known in the annals of mankind.

Rockville Centre, N. Y.
January 1976

Book One

The Sunflower

What was it Arthur said last night? I tried hard to remember. I knew it was very important. If only I were not so tired!

I was standing on the parade-ground, where the prisoners were slowly assembling. They had just had their "breakfast"—a dark, bitter brew which the camp cooks had the nerve to call coffee. The men were still swallowing the stuff as they mustered for the roll-call, anxious not to be late.

I had not fetched my coffee as I did not want to force my way through the crowd. The space in front of the kitchen was a favourite hunting-ground for the many sadists among the SS. They usually hid behind the huts and whenever they felt like it they swooped like birds of prey on to the helpless prisoners. Every day some were injured; it was part of the "programme".

As we stood around silent and gloomy waiting for the order to fall in my thoughts were not concerned with the dangers which always lurked on such occasions, but were entirely centred on last night's talk.

Yes, now I remembered!

It was late at night. We lay in the dark; there were low groans, soft whispering, and an occasional ghostly creak as someone moved on his plank bed. One could hardly discern faces but could easily identify a speaker by his voice. During the day two of the men from our hut had actually been in the Ghetto. The guard officer had given them his permission. An irrational whim? Perhaps inspired by some bribe? I did not know. The likelihood was that it was a mere whim, for what did a prisoner possess to bribe an officer with?

And now the men were making their report.

Arthur huddled up close to them so as not to miss a word. They brought news from outside, war news. I listened half-asleep.

The people in the Ghetto had plenty of information and we in the camp had only a small share of their knowledge. We had to piece bits together from the scanty reports of those who worked outside during the day and overheard what the Poles and Ukrainians were talking about—facts or rumours. Sometimes even people in the street whispered a piece of news to them, from sympathy or as consolation.

Seldom was the news good, and when it was, one questioned if it was really true or merely wishful thinking. Bad news, on the other hand, we accepted unquestioningly; we were so used to it. And one piece of bad news followed another, each more alarming than the last. Today's news was worse than yesterday's, and tomorrow's would be worse still.

The stuffy atmosphere in the hut seemed to stifle thought, as week after week we slept huddled together in the same sweat-sodden clothes that we wore at work during the day. Many of us were so exhausted we did not even take off our boots. From time to time in the night a man would scream in his sleep—a nightmare perhaps, or his neighbour may have kicked him. The hut had once been a stable, and the half-open skylight did not admit enough air to provide oxygen for the hundred and fifty men who lay penned together on the tiers of bunks.

In the polyglot mass of humanity were members of varied social strata; rich and poor; highly educated and illiterate; religious men and agnostics; the kind-hearted and the selfish, courageous men and the dull-witted. A common fate had made them all equal. But inevitably they splintered into small groups, close communities of men who in other circumstances would never be found together.

The group to which I belonged included my old friend Arthur and a Jew named Josek, a recent arrival. These were my closest companions. Josek was sensitive and deeply religious. His faith could be hurt by the environment of the camp and by the jeers or insinuations of others, but it could never be shaken. I, for one, could only envy him. He had an answer for everything, while we others vainly groped for explanations and fell victims to despair. His peace of mind sometimes disconcerted us; Arthur especially, whose attitude to life was ironic, was irritated by Josek's placidity and sometimes he even mocked him or was angry with him.

Jokingly I called Josek "Rabbi". He was not of course a rabbi; he was a business man, but religion permeated his life. He knew that he was superior to us, that we were the poorer for our lack of faith but he was ever ready to share his wealth of wisdom and piety with us and give us strength.

But what consolation was it to know that we were not the first Jews to be persecuted? And what comfort was it when Josek, rummaging among his inexhaustible treasure of anecdotes and legends, proved to us that suffering is the companion of every man from birth onwards?

As soon as Josek spoke, he forgot or ignored his surroundings completely. We had the feeling that he was simply unaware of his position. On one occasion we nearly quarrelled on this point.

It was a Sunday evening. We had stopped work at midday

and lay in our bunks relaxing. Someone was talking about the news; it was of course sad as usual. Josek seemed not to be listening. He asked no questions as the others were doing but suddenly he sat up and his face looked radiant. Then he began to speak.

"Our scholars say that at the Creation of man four angels stood as god-parents. The angels of Mercy, Truth, Peace and Justice. For a long time they disputed as to whether God ought to create man at all. The strongest opponent was the angel of Truth. This angered God and as a punishment He sent him into banishment on earth. But the other angels begged God to pardon him and finally he listened to them and summoned the angel of Truth back to heaven. The angel brought back a clod of earth which was soaked in his tears, tears that he had shed on being banished from heaven. And from this clod of earth the Lord God created man."

Arthur the cynic was vexed and interrupted Josek's discourse.

"Josek," he said, "I am prepared to believe that God created a Jew out of this tear-soaked clod of earth, but do you expect me to believe He also made our camp commandant, Wilhaus, out of the same material?"

"You are forgetting Cain," replied Josek.

"And you are forgetting where you are. Cain slew Abel in anger, but he never tortured him. Cain had a personal attachment to his brother, but we are strangers to our murderers."

I saw at once that Josek was deeply hurt and to prevent a quarrel I joined in the conversation.

"Arthur," I said, "you are forgetting the thousands of years of evolution; what is known as progress."

But both of them merely laughed bitterly—in times like these such platitudes were meaningless.

Arthur's question wasn't altogether unjustified. Were we

truly all made of the same stuff? If so, why were some murderers and other victims? Was there in fact any personal relationship between us, between the murderers and their victims, between our camp commandant, Wilhaus, and a tortured Jew?

And last night I was lying in my bunk half asleep. My back hurt. I felt dizzy as I listened to the voices which seemed to come from far away. I heard something about a piece of news from the BBC in London—or from Radio Moscow.

Suddenly Arthur gripped my shoulder and shook me.

"Simon, do you hear?" he cried.

"Yes," I murmured, "I hear."

"I hope you are listening with your ears, for your eyes are half closed, and you really must hear what the old woman said."

"Which old woman?" I asked. "I thought you were talking about what you had heard from the BBC?"

"That was earlier. You must have dozed off. The old woman was saying . . ."

"What could she have said? Does she know when we will get out of here? Or when they are going to slaughter us?"

"Nobody knows the answers to those questions. But she said something else, something that we should perhaps think about in times like these. She thought that God was on leave." Arthur paused for a moment in order to let the words sink in. "What do you think of that, Simon?" he asked. "God is on leave."

"Let me sleep," I replied. "Tell me when He gets back."

For the first time since we had been living in the stable I heard my friends laughing, or had I merely dreamt it?

We were still waiting for the order to fall in. Apparently

there was some sort of hitch. So I had time to ask Arthur how much of what I recalled was dream and how much real.

"Arthur," I asked, "what were we talking about last night? About God? About 'God on leave'?"

"Josek was in the Ghetto yesterday. He asked an old woman for news, but she only looked up to heaven and said seriously: 'Oh God Almighty, come back from your leave and look at Thy earth again'."

"So that's the news; we live in a world that God has abandoned?" I commented.

I had known Arthur for years, since the time when I was a young architect and he was both my adviser and my friend. We were like brothers, he a lawyer and writer with a perpetual ironic smile around the corners of his mouth, while I had gradually become resigned to the idea that I would never again build houses in which people would live in freedom and happiness. Our thoughts in the prison camp often ran on different lines. Arthur was already living in another world and imagined things that would probably not happen for years. True, he did not believe that we could survive, but he was convinced that in the last resort the Germans would not escape unpunished. They would perhaps succeed in killing us and millions of other innocent people, but they themselves would thereby be destroyed.

I lived more in the present: savouring hunger, exhaustion, anxiety for my family, humiliations . . . most of all humiliations.

I once read somewhere that it is impossible to break a man's firm belief. If I ever thought that true, life in a concentration camp taught me differently. It is impossible to believe anything in a world that has ceased to regard man as man, which repeatedly 'proves' that one is no longer a man. So one begins to doubt, one begins to cease to believe in a world order in which God has a definite place. One really begins to think that God is on leave. Otherwise the present state of things wouldn't be possible. God must be away. And He has no deputy.

What the old woman had said in no way shocked me, she had simply stated what I had long felt to be true.

We had been back in the camp again for a week. The guards at the Eastern Railway works had carried out a fresh "registration". These registrations involved new dangers that were quite unimaginable in normal life. The oftener they registered us, the fewer we became. In SS language, registering was not a mere stocktaking. It meant much more; the redistribution of labour, culling the men who were no longer essential workers and throwing them out—usually into the death chamber. From bitter personal experience we mistrusted words whose natural meaning seemed harmless. The Germans' intentions towards us had never been harmless. We were suspicious of everything and with good reason.

Until a short time ago about two hundred of us had been employed at the Eastern Railway works. Work there was far from light, but we felt free to some extent and did not need to return to the camp each night. Our food was brought from the camp, and it tasted accordingly. But as the guards were railway police we were not continually exposed to the unpredictable whims of the SS camp patrols.

The Germans looked on many of the overseers and foremen as second-class citizens. The ethnic Germans were better treated, but the Poles and Ukrainians formed a special stratum between the self-appointed German supermen and the sub-human Jews, and already they were trembling at the thought of the day when there would be no Jews left. Then the well-oiled machinery of extermination would be turned in their direction. The ethnic Germans too did not always feel comfortable and some of them betrayed their uneasiness by behaving more "German" than the average German. A few showed sympathy towards us by slipping us pieces of bread on the quiet and seeing to it that we were not worked to death.

Among those who demanded a daily stint in cruelty was an elderly drunkard called Delosch, who, when he had nothing to drink, passed the time by beating up the prisoners. The group he guarded often bribed him with money to buy liquor, and sometimes a prisoner would try to enlist his maudlin sympathy by describing the fate of the Jews. It worked when he was sufficiently "under the influence". His bullying was as notorious in the works as his pet witticism. When he learned that some prisoner's family had been exterminated in the Ghetto Delosch's invariable response was: "There will always be a thousand Jews left to attend the funeral of the last Jew in Lemberg." We heard this several times a day and Delosch was immensely proud of this particular wisecrack.

By the time the various groups had formed up on the command to fall-in, we who longed for outside work had already resigned ourselves to the prospect of remaining in the camp. In the camp construction work went on without interruption, and every day there were deaths in the camp; Jews were strung up, trampled under foot, bitten by trained dogs, whipped, and humiliated in every conceivable manner. Many who could bear it no longer voluntarily put an end to their lives. They sacrificed a number of days, weeks, or months of their lives, but they saved themselves countless brutalities and tortures.

Staying in camp meant that one was guarded not by a single SS man but by many, and often the guards amused themselves by wandering from one workshop to another, whipping prisoners indiscriminately, or reporting them to the commandant for alleged sabotage, which always led to dire punishment. If an SS man alleged that a prisoner was not working properly, his word was accepted, even if the prisoner could point to the work he had done. What an SS man said was always right.

The work assignment was almost finished and we from the Eastern Railway works stood around despondently. Apparently we were no longer wanted on the railway. Then suddenly a corporal came over to us and counted off fifty men. I was among these, but Arthur was left behind. We were formed up in threes, marched through the inner gate where six "askaris" were assigned us as guards. These were Russian deserters or prisoners who had enlisted for service under the Germans. The term "askari" was used during the First World War to describe the negro soldier employed by the Germans in East Africa. For some reason the SS used the name for the Russian auxiliaries. They were employed in concentration camps to assist the guards and they knew only too well what the Germans expected from them. And most of them lived up to expectations. Their brutality was only mitigated by their corruptibility. The "kapos" (camp captains) and foremen kept on fairly good terms with them, providing them with liquor and cigarettes. So outside working parties were thus able to enjoy a greater degree of liberty under the guardianship of the askaris.

Strangely enough the askaris were extremely keen on singing: music in general played an important part in camp life. There was even a band. Its members included some of the best musicians in and around Lemberg. Richard Rokita, the SS lieutenant who had been a violinist in a Silesian café was mad about "his" band. This man, who daily slaughtered prisoners from sheer lust for killing had at the same time only one ambition—to lead a band. He arranged special accommodation for his musicians and pampered them in other ways, but they were never allowed out of camp. In the evenings they played works of Bach, and Wagner and Grieg. One day Rokita brought along a song-writer called Zygmunt Schlechter and ordered him to compose a "death tango". And whenever the band played this tune, the sadistic monster Rokita had wet eyes.

In the early mornings, when the prisoners left the camp to go to work, the band played them out, the SS insisting that we march in time to the music. When we passed the gate we began to sing.

The camp songs were of a special type, a mixture of melancholy, sick humour and vulgar words, a weird amalgam of Russian, Polish and German. The obscenities suited the mentality of the askaris who constantly demanded one particular song. When they heard it broad grins came over their faces and their features lost some of their brutal appearance.

Once we had passed beyond the barbed wire, the air seemed fresher; people and houses were no longer seen through wire mesh and partly hidden by the watch towers.

Pedestrians often stood and stared at us curiously and sometimes they started to wave but soon desisted, fearing the SS might notice the gesture of friendliness.

Traffic on the streets seemed uninfluenced by the war. The front line was seven miles away, and the presence of a few soldiers was the only reminder that it was not peace time.

One askari began to sing, and we joined in although few of us were in the mood for singing. Women among the gaping passers-by turned their heads away shamefacedly when they heard the obscene pasages in the song and naturally this delighted the askaris. One of them left the column, ran over to the pavement to accost a girl. We couldn't hear what he said, but we could well imagine it as the girl blushed and walked rapidly away.

Our gaze roamed the crowds on the pavements looking anxiously for any face we might recognise. Although some kept eyes on the ground, fearing to encounter an acquaintance.

You could read on the faces of the passers-by that we were written off as doomed. The people of Lemberg had become accustomed to the sight of tortured Jews and they looked at us as one looks at a herd of cattle being driven to the slaughter house. At such times I was consumed by a feeling that the world had conspired against us and our fate was accepted without a protest, without a trace of sympathy.

I for one no longer wanted to look at the indifferent faces of the spectators. Did any of them reflect that there were still Jews and as long as they were there, as long as the Nazis were still busy with the Jews, they would leave the citizens alone? I suddenly remembered an experience I had had a few days before, not far from here. As we were returning to camp, a man whom I had formerly known passed by, a fellow student, now a Polish engineer. Perhaps understandably he was afraid to nod to me openly, but I could see from the expression in his eyes that he was surprised to see me still alive. For him we were as good as dead; each of us was carrying around his own death certificate, from which only the date was missing.

Our column suddenly came to a halt at a crossroads.

I could see nothing that might be holding us up but I noticed on the left of the street there was a military cemetery. It was enclosed by a low barbed wire fence. The wires were threaded through sparse bushes and low shrubs, but between them you could see the graves aligned in stiff rows.

And on each grave there was planted a sunflower, as straight as a soldier on parade.

I stared spellbound. The flower heads seemed to absorb the sun's rays like mirrors and draw them down into the darkness of the ground as my gaze wandered from the sunflower to the grave. It seemed to penetrate the earth and suddenly I saw before me a periscope. It was gaily coloured and butterflies fluttered from flower to flower. Were they carrying messages from grave to grave? Were they whispering something to each flower to pass on to the soldier below? Yes, this was just what they were doing; the dead were receiving light and messages.

Suddenly I envied the dead soldiers. Each had a sunflower to connect him with the living world, and butterflies to visit his grave. For me there would be no sunflower. I would be buried in a mass-grave, where corpses would be piled on top of me. No sunflower would ever bring light into my darkness, and no butterflies would dance above my dreadful tomb.

I do not know how long we stood there. The man behind gave me a push and the procession started again. As we walked on I still had my head turned towards the sunflowers. They were countless and indistinguishable one from another. But the men who were buried under them had not severed all connection with the world. Even in death they were superior to us . . .

I rarely thought of death. I knew that it was waiting for me and must come sooner or later, so gradually I had accustomed myself to its proximity. I was not even curious as to how it would come. There were too many possibilities. All I hoped was that it would be quick. Just how it would happen I left to Fate.

But for some strange reason the sight of the sunflowers had aroused new thoughts in me. I felt I would come across them again; that they were a symbol with a special meaning for me.

As we reached Janowska Street, leaving the cemetery behind us, I turned my head for a last look at the forest of sunflowers.

We still did not know where we were being taken. My neighbour whispered to me: "Perhaps they have set up new workshops in the Ghetto."

It was possible. The rumour was that new workshops were being started. More and more German businessmen were settling in Lemberg. They were not so anxious for profits. It was more important for them to keep their employees and save them from military service which was comparatively easy in peaceful Lemberg, far from the front line. What most of these enterprises brought with them from Germany was writing paper, a rubber stamp, a few foremen and some office furniture. Only a short time ago Lemberg had been in the hands of the Russians, who had nationalised most of the building firms, many of which had previously been owned by Jews. When the Russians withdrew, they were unable to take the machines and tools with them. So what they left behind was taken to a "booty depot" and was now being divided among the newly established German factories.

There was no trouble in any case about getting labour. So long as there were still Jews, one could get cheap, almost free labour. The workshop applying, had merely to be recognised as important for the war, but a certain degree of protection and bribery was also necessary. Those with connections got permission to set up branches in occupied territory, they were given cheap labour in the shape of hundreds of Jews, and they also had an extensive machine depot at their disposal. The men they brought with them from Germany were exempt from active service. Homes in the German quarter of Lemberg were assigned to them—very nice houses abandoned by wealthy Poles and Jews to make room for the master race.

To the Jews it was an advantage that so many German enterprises were being started in Poland. Work was not particularly hard, and as a rule the workshop managers fought for "their" Jews, without whose cheap labour the workshops would have had to move further east nearer the front.

All around me I heard the anxious whispers: "Where are we going?"

"Going" means to carry out with the feet a decision which the brain has formed, but in our case our brains made no decisions. Our feet merely imitated what the front man did. They stopped when he stopped and they moved on when he moved on.

We turned right into Janowska Street; how often had I sauntered along it, as a student and later as an architect? For a time I had even had lodgings there with a fellow student from Przemysl.

Now we marched mechanically along the street—a column of doomed men.

It was not yet eight o'clock, but there was already plenty of traffic. Peasants were coming into the city to barter their wares; they no longer had confidence in money as is always the case in war time and in crises. The peasants paid no attention to our column.

As we moved out of the city the askaris, having sung themselves hoarse, were taking a rest. Detrained soldiers with their baggage hurried along Janowska; SS men passed, looking contemptuously at us, and at one point an army officer stopped to stare. Around his neck hung a camera, but he could not make up his mind to use it on us. Hesitatingly he passed the camera from right to left hand and then let it go again. Perhaps he was afraid of trouble with the SS.

We came in sight of the church at the end of Janowska Street, a lofty structure of red brick and squared stone. Which direction would the askari, at the head of our column, take? To the right, down to the station, or to the left along Sapiehy Street, at the end of which lay the notorious Loncki Prison?

We turned left.

I knew the way well. In Sapiehy Street stood the Technical High School. For years I had walked along this street several times a day, when I was working for the Polish diploma.

Even then for us Jewish students Sapiehy Street was a street of doom. Only a few Jewish families lived there and in times of disorder the district was avoided by Jews. Here lived Poles—regular officers, professional men, manufacturers and officials. Their sons were known as the "gilded youth" of Lemberg and supplied most of the students in the Technical High School and in the High School of Agriculture. Many of them were rowdies, hooligans, anti-semites, and Jews who fell into their hands were often beaten up and left bleeding on the ground. They fastened razor blades to the end of their sticks which they used as weapons against the Jewish students. In the evenings it was dangerous to walk through this street, even if one were merely Jewish in appearance, especially at times when the young National Democrats or Radical Nationals were turning their anti-Jewish slogans from theory into practice. It was rare for a policeman to be around to protect the victims.

What was incomprehensible, was that at a time when Hitler was on Poland's western frontiers, poised to annexe Polish territory, these Polish "patriots" could think of only one thing: the Jews and their hatred for them.

In Germany, at that time, they were building new factories to raise armament potential to the maximum; they were building strategic roads straight towards Poland and then were calling up more and more young Germans for military service. But the Polish parliament paid little heed to this menace; it had "more important" tasks—new regulations for kosher butchering for instance—which might make life more difficult for the Jews.

Such parliamentary debates were always followed by street battles, for the Jewish intelligensia was ever a thorn in the flesh of the anti-semites.

Two years before the outbreak of war the Radical elements had invented a "day without Jews", whereby they hoped to reduce the number of Jewish academics, to interfere with their studies and make it impossible for them to take examinations. On these feast days there assembled inside the gates of the High Schools a crowd of fraternity students wearing ribbons incribed "the day without the Jews". It always coincided with examination days. The "day without the Jews" was thus a movable festival, and as the campus of the Technical High School was ex-territorial, the police were not allowed to interfere except by express request of the Rector. Such requests were rarely made. Although the Radicals formed a mere twenty per cent of the students, this minority reigned because of the cowardice and laziness of the majority. The great mass of the students were unconcerned about the Jews or indeed about order and justice. They were not willing to expose themselves, they lacked will-power, they were wrapped up in their own problems, completely indifferent to the fate of Jewish students.

The proportions were about the same among the teaching staff. Some were confirmed anti-semites, but even from those who were not, the Jewish students had trouble getting a substitute date for the examinations which they missed because of the "day without Jews" outbreaks. For Jews who came from poor families the loss of a term meant inevitably an end to their studies. So they had to go to the High School even on the anti-semitic feast days and this led to grotesque situations. In the side streets ambulances waited patiently and they had plenty to do on examination days. The police too waited to prevent violence from spreading outside the campus. From time to time a few of the most brutal students were arrested and tried but they emerged from prison as heroes and on their lapels they proudly wore a badge designed as a prison gate. They had suffered for their country's cause! Honoured by their comrades, they were given special privileges by some of the professors, and never was there any question of expelling them.

Such memories crowded into my mind as, under the guard of the askaris, I marched past the familiar houses. I looked into the faces of the passers-by. Perhaps I would see a former fellow-student. I would spot him at once because he would visibly show the hatred and contempt which they always evinced at the mere sight of a Jew. I had seen this expression too often during my time as student ever to forget it.

Where are they now, these super-patriots who dreamt of a "Poland without Jews"? Perhaps the day when there would be no more Jews was not far off, and their dreams would be realised. Only there wouldn't be a Poland either!

We halted in front of the Technical High School. It looked unaltered. The main building, a neo-classic structure in terra-cotta and yellow, stood some distance back from the street, from which it was separated by a low stone wall with a high iron fence. At examination time I had often walked along this fence and gazed through the railings at the Radical students waiting for their victims. Over the broad entrance gates would be a banner inscribed "the day without Jews". From the gate to the door of the building armed students forming a cordon, would scrutinise everybody who wanted to enter the building.

So here I was, once again standing outside this gateway. This time there were no banners, no students to make the Jews run the gauntlet, only a few German guards and, above the entrance, a board inscribed "Reserve Hospital". An SS man from the camp had a few words with a sentry, and then the gate opened. We marched past the well-kept lawns, turned left from the main entrance and were led round the building into the courtyard. It lay in deep shadow. Ambulances drove in and out, and once or twice we had to stand aside to let them pass. Then we were handed over to a sergeant of the medical corps, who assigned us our duties. I had a curious feeling of strangeness in these surroundings although I had spent several years here. I tried to remember whether I had ever been in this back courtyard. What would have brought me here? We were usually content to be able to get into the building and out again without being molested, or without explaining the topography.

Large concrete containers were arranged around the courtyard and they seemed to be filled with blood-stained bandages. The ground was covered with empty boxes, sacks and packing material which a group of prisoners was busy loading into trucks. The air stank with a mixture of strong-smelling medicaments, disinfectants and putrefaction.

Red Cross sisters and medical orderlies were hurrying to and fro. The askaris had left the shady smelly courtyard and were sunning themselves on the grass a short distance away. Some were rolling cigarettes of newspaper stuffed with tobacco—just as they were wont to do in Russia.

Some lightly wounded and convalescent soldiers sat on the benches, watching the askaris, whom they recognised at once as Russians in spite of the German uniforms they wore. We could hear them inquiring about us too.

One soldier got up from the bench and came over towards us. He looked at us in an impersonal way as if we were animals in a zoo. Probably he was wondering how long we had to live. Then he pointed to his arm, which was in a sling, and called out: "You Jewish swine, that's what your brothers the damned Communists have done for me. But you'll soon kick the bucket, all of you."

The other soldiers didn't seem to share his views. They looked at us sympathetically and one of them shook his head doubtfully; but none dared to say a word. The soldier who had approached us uttered a few more curses and then sat down again in the sunshine.

I thought to myself that this vile creature would one day have a sunflower planted on his grave to watch over him. I looked at him closely and all at once I saw only the sunflower. My stare seemed to upset him for he picked up a stone and threw it at me. The stone missed and the sunflower vanished. At that moment I felt desperately alone and wished Arthur had been included in my group.

The orderly in charge of us finally led us away. Our job was to carry cartons filled with rubbish out of the building. Their contents apparently came from the operating theatres and the stench made one's throat contract.

As I stepped aside to get a few breaths of clean air, I noticed a small, plump nurse who wore the grey-blue uniform with white facings and the regulation white cap. She looked at me curiously and then came straight over to me.

"Are you a Jew?" she asked.

I looked at her wonderingly. Why did she ask, could not she see it for herself from my clothes and my features? Was she trying to be insulting? What was the object of her question?

A sympathetic soul perhaps, I thought. Maybe she wanted to slip me some bread, and was afraid to do it here with the others looking on.

Two months previously when I was working on the Eastern Railway, loading oxygen cylinders, a soldier had climbed out of a truck on a siding close by and come over to me. He said he had been watching us for some time, and we looked as if we did not get enough to eat.

"In my knapsack over there you'll find a piece of bread; go and fetch it."

I asked, "Why don't you give it to me yourself?"

"It is forbidden to give anything to a Jew."

"I know," I said. "All the same if you want me to have it you give it to me."

He smiled. "No, you take it. Then I can swear with a clear conscience that I didn't give it to you."

I thought of this incident as I followed the Red Cross nurse into the building, in accordance with her instructions.

The thick walls made the inside of the building refreshingly cool. The nurse walked rather fast. Where was she taking me? If her purpose was to give me something, then she could have done it here and now in front of the staircase, since nobody was in sight. But the nurse just turned round once, to confirm that I was still following her.

We climbed the staircase, and, strange to relate I could not remember ever having seen it before. At the next storey I saw nurses were coming towards us and a doctor looked at me sharply as if to say: What is that fellow doing here?

We reached the upper hall, where, not so long ago, my diploma had been handed to me.

The nurse stopped and exchanged a few words with another nurse. I asked myself whether I had better bolt. I was on well-known ground. I knew where each corridor led to and could easily escape. Let her look for somebody else, whatever it was she needed.

Suddenly I forgot why I was there. I forgot the nurse and even the camp. There on the right was the way to Professor Bagierski's office and there on the left the way to Professor Derdacki's. Both were notorious for their dislike of Jewish students. I had done my diploma work with Derdacki—a design for a sanatorium. And Bagierski had corrected many of my essays. When he had to deal with a Jewish student he seemed to lose his breath and stuttered more than usual. I could still see his hand making lines across my drawings with a thick pencil, a hand with a large signet ring.

Then the nurse signalled me to wait, and I came back to earth. I leant over the balustrade and looked down at the busy throng in the lower hall. Wounded were being brought in on stretchers. There was a constant coming and going. Soldiers limped past on crutches and one soldier on a stretcher looked up at me, his features distorted with pain.

Then another fragment from the past recurred to my memory. It was during the student riots of 1936. The anti-semitic bands had hurled a Jewish student over the balustrade into the lower hall and he lay there just like this soldier, possibly on the very same spot.

Just past the balustrade was a door which had led to the office of the Dean of Architecture and it was here we handed in our exercise books to the Professors to be marked. The Dean in my time was a quiet man, very polite, very correct. We had never known whether he was for or against the Jews. He always responded to our greetings with distant politeness. One could almost physically feel his aloofness. Or was it merely an excess of sensitiveness that made us divide people into two groups: those that liked Jews and those who disliked them. Constant Jew-baiting gave rise to such thoughts.

The nurse came back and dragged me once again out of the past. I could see from the look in her eyes that she was pleased to find me still there.

She walked quickly along the balustrade around the hall and stopped in front of the door of the Dean's room.

"Wait here till I call you."

I nodded and looked up the staircase. Orderlies were bringing down a motionless figure on a stretcher. There had never been a lift in the building and the Germans had not installed one. After a few moments the nurse came out of the Dean's room, caught me by the arm and pushed me through the door.

I looked for the familiar objects, the writing desk, the cupboards in which our papers were kept, but those relics of the past had vanished. There was now only a white bed with a night table beside it. Something white was looking at me out of the blankets. At first I could not grasp the situation.

Then the nurse bent over the bed and whispered and I heard a somewhat deeper whisper, apparently in answer. Although the place was in semi-darkness I could now see a figure wrapped in white, motionless on the bed. I tried to trace the outlines of the body under the sheets and looked for its head.

The nurse straightened up and said quietly: "Stay here." Then she went out of the room.

From the bed I heard a weak, broken voice exclaim: "Please come nearer, I can't speak loudly."

Now I could see the figure in the bed far more clearly. White, bloodless hands on the counterpane, head completely bandaged with openings only for mouth, nose and ears. The feeling of unreality persisted. It was an uncanny situation. Those corpse-like hands, the bandages, and the place in which this strange encounter was taking place.

I did not know who this wounded man was, but obviously he was a German.

Hesitatingly, I sat down on the edge of the bed. The sick man, perceiving this, said softly: "Please come a little nearer, to talk loudly is exhausting."

I obeyed. His almost bloodless hand groped for mine as he tried to raise himself slightly in the bed.

My bewilderment was intense. I did not know whether this unreal scene was actuality or dream. Here was I in the ragged clothes of a concentration camp prisoner in the room of the former Dean of Lemberg High School—now a military hospital—in a sick room which must be in reality a death chamber.

As my eyes became accustomed to the semi-darkness I could see that the white bandages were mottled with yellow stains. Perhaps ointment, or was it pus? The bandaged head was spectral.

I sat on the bed spellbound. I could not take my eyes off the stricken man and the grey-yellow stains on the bandages seemed to me to be moving, taking new shapes before my eyes.

"I have not much longer to live," whispered the sick man in a barely audible voice. "I know the end is near."

Then he fell silent. Was he thinking what next to say, or had his premonition of death scared him? I looked more closely. He was very thin, and under his shirt his bones were clearly visible, almost bursting through his parched skin.

I was unmoved by his words. The way I had been forced to exist in the prison camps had destroyed in me any feeling or fear about death.

Sickness, suffering and doom were the constant companions of us Jews. Such things no longer frightened us.

Nearly a fortnight before this confrontation with the dying man I had had occasion to visit a store in which cement sacks were kept. I heard groans and going to investigate, I saw one of the prisoners lying among the sacks. I asked him what was the matter.

"I am dying," he muttered in a choked voice, "I shall die;

there is nobody in the world to help me and nobody to mourn my death." Then he added casually, "I am twenty-two."

I ran out of the shed and found the prison doctor. He shrugged his shoulders and turned away. "There are a couple of hundred men working here today. Six of them are dying." He did not even ask where the dying man was.

"You ought at least to go and look at him," I protested.

"I couldn't do anything for him." he answered.

"But you as a doctor have more liberty to move about, you could explain your absence to the guards better than I could. It is frightful for a man to die lonely and abandoned. Help him at least in his dying hour."

"Good, good," he said. But I knew that he would not go. He too had lost all feeling for death.

At the evening roll-call there were six corpses. They were included without comment. The doctor's estimate was correct.

"I know," muttered the sick man, "that at this moment thousands of men are dying. Death is everywhere. It is neither infrequent nor extraordinary. I am resigned to dying soon, but before that I want to talk about an experience which is torturing me. Otherwise I cannot die in peace."

He was breathing heavily. I had the feeling that he was staring at me through his head bandage. Perhaps he could see through the yellow stains, although they were nowhere near his eyes. I could not look at him.

"I heard from one of the sisters that there were Jewish prisoners working in the courtyard. Previously she had brought me a letter from my mother . . . She read it out to me and then went away. I have been here for three months. Then I came to a decision. After thinking it over for a long time . . .

"When the sister came back I asked her to help me. I wanted her to fetch a Jewish prisoner to me, but I warned she must be careful that nobody must see her. The nurse, who had no idea why I had made this request didn't reply and went away. I gave up all hope of her taking such a risk for my sake. But when she came in a little while ago she bent over me and whispered that there was a Jew outside. She said it as if complying with the last wish of a dying man. She knows how it is with me. I am in a death chamber, that I know. They let the hopeless cases die alone. Perhaps they don't want the others to be upset."

Who was this man to whom I was listening? What was he trying to say to me? Was he a Jew who had camouflaged himself as a German and now, on his deathbed, wanted to look at a Jew again? According to gossip in the Ghetto and later in the camp there were Jews in Germany who were "Aryan" in appearance and had enlisted in the army with false papers. They had even got into the SS. That was their method of survival. Was this man such a Jew? Or perhaps a half-Jew, son of a mixed marriage? When he made a slight movement I noticed that his other hand rested on a letter but which now slipped to the floor. I bent down and put it back on the counterpane.

I didn't touch his hand and he could not have seen my movement—nevertheless he reacted.

"Thank you—that is my mother's letter," the words came softly from his lips.

And again I had the feeling he was staring at me.

His hand groped for the letter and drew it towards him, as if he hoped to derive a little strength and courage from contact with the paper. I thought of my own mother who would never write me another letter. Five weeks previously she had been dragged out of the Ghetto in a raid. The only article of

33

value which we still possessed, after all the looting, was a gold watch which I had given to my mother so that she might be able to buy herself off when they came to fetch her. A neighbour who had valid papers told me later what had happened to the watch. My mother gave it to the Ukrainian policeman who came to arrest her. He went away, but soon came back and bundled my mother and others into a truck, that carried them away to a place from which no letters ever emerged . . .

Time seemed to stand still, as I listened to the croaking of the dying man.

"My name is Karl . . . I joined the SS as a volunteer. Of course—when you hear the word SS . . ."

He stopped. His throat seemed to be dry and he tried hard to swallow a lump in it.

Now I knew he couldn't be a Jew or half-Jew who had hidden inside a German uniform. How could I have imagined such a thing? But in those days anything was possible.

"I must tell you something dreadful . . . Something inhuman. It happened a year ago—has a year already gone by?" These last words he spoke almost to himself.

"Yes, it is a year," he continued, "a year since the crime I committed. I have to talk to someone about it, perhaps that will help."

Then his hand grasped mine. His fingers clutched mine tightly, as though he sensed I was trying unconsciously to withdraw my hand when I heard the word "crime". Whence had he derived the strength? Or was it that I was so weak that I could not take my hand away?

"I must tell you of this horrible deed—tell you because . . . you are a Jew."

Could there be some kind of horror unknown to us?

All the atrocities and tortures that a sick brain can invent are familiar to me. I have felt them on my own body and I have seen them happen in the camp. Any story that this sick man had to tell couldn't surpass the horror stories which my comrades in the camp exchanged with each other at night.

I wasn't really curious about his story, and inwardly I only hoped the nurse had remembered to tell an askari where I was. Otherwise they would be looking for me. Perhaps they would think I had escaped . . .

I was uneasy. I could hear voices outside the door, but I recognised one as the nurse's voice and that reassured me. The strangled voice went on: "Some time elapsed before I realised what guilt I had incurred."

I stared at the bandaged head. I didn't know what he wanted to confess, but I knew for sure that after his death a sunflower would grow on his grave. Already a sunflower was turning towards the window, the window through which the sun was sending its rays into this death chamber. Why was the sunflower already making its appearance? Because it would accompany him to the cemetery, stand on his grave and sustain his connection with life. And this I envied him. I envied him also because in his last moments he was able to think of a live mother who would be grieving for him.

"I was not born a murderer . . ." he wheezed.

He breathed heavily and was silent.

"I come from Stuttgart and I am now twenty-one. That is too soon to die. I have had very little out of life."

Of course it is too soon to die I thought. But did the Nazis ask whether our children whom they were about to gas had ever had anything out of life? Did they ask whether it was too soon for them to die? Certainly nobody had ever asked me the question.

As if he had guessed my mental reaction he said: "I know what you are thinking and I understand. But may I not still say that I am too young . . . ?"

Then in a burst of calm coherency he went on: "My father who was manager of a factory was a convinced Social Democrat. After 1933 he got into difficulties, but that happened to many. My mother brought me up as a Catholic, I was actually a server in the church and a special favourite of our priest who hoped I would one day study theology. But it turned out differently; I joined the Hitler Youth, and that of course was the end of the Church for me. My mother was very sad, but finally stopped reproaching me. I was her only child. My father never uttered a word on the subject . . .

"He was afraid lest I should talk in the Hitler Youth about what I had heard at home . . . Our leader demanded that we should champion our cause everywhere . . . Even at home . . . He told us that if we heard anyone abuse it we must report to him. There were many who did so, but not I. My parents nevertheless were afraid and they stopped talking when I was near. Their mistrust annoyed me, but, unfortunately, there was no time for reflection in those days.

"In the Hitler Youth, I found friends and comrades. My days were full. After school most of our class hurried to the clubhouse or sports ground. My father rarely spoke to me, and when he had something to say he spoke cautiously and with reserve. I know now what depressed him—often I watched him sitting in his armchair for hours, brooding, without saying a word . . .

"When the war broke out I volunteered, naturally in the SS. I was far from being the only one in my troop to do so; almost half of them joined the forces voluntarily—without a thought, as if they were going to a dance or on an outing. My mother wept when I left. As I closed the door behind me I heard my father say: 'They are taking our son away from us. No good will come of it.'

"His words made me indignant. I wanted to go back and

argue with him. I wanted to tell him that he simply did not understand modern times. But I let it be, so as not to make my departure worse for all of us by an ugly scene.

"Those words were the last I ever heard my father speak . . . Occasionally he would add a few lines to my mother's letter but my mother usually made excuses by saying he was not back from work and she was anxious to catch the post."

He paused, and groped with his hand for the glass on the night table. Although he could not see it he knew where it was. He drank a mouthful of water and put the glass back safely in its place before I could do it for him. Was he really in such a bad way as he had said?

"We were first sent to a training camp at an army base where we listened feverishly to the radio messages about the Polish campaign. We devoured the reports in the newspapers and dreaded that our services might not after all be needed. I was longing for experience, to see the world, to be able to recount my adventures . . . My uncle had had such exciting tales to tell of the war in Russia, how they had driven Ivan into the Masurian Lakes. I wanted to play my part in that sort of thing . . ."

I sat there like a cat on hot bricks and tried to release my hand from his. I wanted to go away, but he seemed to be trying to talk to me with his hand as well as his voice. His grip grew tighter—as if pleading with me not to desert him. Perhaps his hand was a replacement for his eyes.

I looked round the room and glancing at the window, I saw a part of the sun-drenched courtyard, with the shadow of the roof crossing it obliquely—a boundary between light and dark, a defined boundary without any transition.

Then the dying man told of his time in occupied Poland, mentioning a place. Was it Reichshof? I didn't ask.

Why the long prelude? Why didn't he say what he wanted from me. There was no necessity to break it so gently.

Now his hand began to tremble and I took the opportunity to withdraw mine, but he clutched it again and whispered: "Please." Did he want to fortify himself—or me?—for what was to come?

"And then—then came the terrible thing . . . But first I must tell you a little more about myself."

He seemed to detect my uneasiness. Had he noticed I was watching the door for suddenly he said:

"No one will come in. The nurse promised to keep watch out there . . .

"Heinz, my schoolmate, who was with me in Poland too, always called me a dreamer. I didn't really know why, perhaps because I was always merry and happy—at least until that day came and it happened . . . It's a good thing that Heinz cannot hear me now. My mother must never know what I did. She must not lose her image of a good son. That is what she always called me. She must always see me as she wanted to see me.

"She used to read my letters out to all the neighbours . . . and the neighbours said that they were proud I got my wound fighting for the Führer and the Fatherland . . . you know the usual phrase . . ."

His voice grew bitter as if he wanted to hurt himself, give himself pain.

"In my mother's memory I am still a happy boy without a care in the world . . . Full of high spirits. Oh, the jokes we used to play . . ."

As he recalled his youth and comrades, I too thought back on the years when practical jokes were a hobby of mine. I thought of my old friends—my schoolmates in Prague. We had had many a joke together, we who were young with life stretching before us.

But what had my youth in common with his? Were we not from different worlds? Where were the friends from my world? Still in camp or already in a nameless mass grave . . . And where are his friends? They are alive, or at least they have a sunflower on their graves and a cross with their name on it.

And now I began to ask myself why a Jew must listen to the confession of a dying Nazi soldier. If he had really rediscovered his faith in Christianity, then a priest should have been sent for, a priest who could help him to die in peace. If I were dying to whom should I make my confession if indeed I had anything to confess? And any way I would not have as much time as this man had. My end would be violent, as had happened to millions before me. Perhaps it would be an unexpected surprise, perhaps I would have no time to prepare for the bullet. He was still talking about his youth as if he were reading aloud and the only effect was that it made me think of my youth too. But it was so far away that it seemed unreal. It seemed as if I had always been in prison camps, as though I were born merely to be maltreated by beasts in human shape who wanted to work off their frustrations and racial hatreds on defenceless victims. Remembrance of time past only made me feel weak, and I badly needed to remain strong for only the strong in these dire times had a hope of survival. I still clung to the belief that the world one day would revenge itself on these brutes—in spite of their victories, their jubilation at the battles they had won, and their boundless arrogance. The day would surely come when the Nazis would hang their heads as the Jews did now . . .

All my instincts were against continuing to listen to this deathbed disavowal. I wanted to get away. The dying man must have felt this, for he dropped the letter and groped for my arm. The movement was so pathetically helpless that all of a sudden I felt sorry for him. I would stay, although I wanted to go. Quietly he continued talking.

"Last spring we saw that something was afoot. We were told time after time we must be prepared for great doings. Each of us must show himself a man . . . He must be tough. There was no place for humanitarian nonsense. The Führer needed real men. That made a great impression on us at the time.

"When the war with Russia began, we listened over the radio to a speech by Himmler before we marched out. He spoke of the final victory of the Führer's mission . . . On smoking out sub-humans . . . We were given piles of literature about the Jews and the Bolsheviks, we devoured the "Sturmer", and many cut caricatures from it and pinned them above our beds. But that was not the sort of thing I cared for . . . In the evenings, in the canteen we grew heated with beer and talk about Germany's future. As in Poland, the war with Russia would be a lightning campaign, thanks to the genius of our leader. Our frontiers would be pushed further and further eastwards. The German people needed room to live."

For a moment he stopped as though exhausted.

"You can see for yourself on what sort of career my life was launched."

He was sorry for himself. His words were bitter and resigned.

I again looked through the window and perceived that the boundary between light and shadow was now above the other windows of the inner façade. The sun had climbed higher. One of the windows caught the sun's rays and reflected them as it was closed again. For a moment the flash of light looked like a heliographic signal. At that time we were ready to see symbols in everything. It was a time rife for mysticism and superstition. Often my fellow prisoners in the camp told ghost stories. Everything for us was unreal and insubstantial: the earth was peopled with mystical shapes; God was on leave, and in His absence others had taken over, to give us signs and hints. In normal times we would have laughed at anybody who believed in supernatural powers. But nowadays we expected them to intervene in the course of events. We devoured every word spoken by alleged soothsayers and fortune-tellers. We often clung to completely nonsensical interpretations if only they gave us a ray of hope for better times. The eternal optimism of the Jew surpassed all reason, but now even reason was out of place. What in this Nazi world was reasonable and logical? You lost yourself in fantasy merely in order to escape from the appalling truth. And in such circumstances reason would have been a barrier. We escaped into dreams and we didn't want to awake from those dreams.

I forgot for a moment where I was and then I heard a buzzing sound. A bluebottle, probably attracted by the smell, flew round the head of the dying man who could not see it nor could he see me wave it away.

"Thanks," he nevertheless whispered. And for the first time I realised that I, a defenceless sub-human, had contrived to lighten the lot of an equally defenceless superman, without thinking, simply as a matter of course.

The narration proceeded: "At the end of June we joined a unit of storm troops and were taken to the front in trucks. We drove past vast fields of wheat which stretched as far as the eye could see. Our platoon leader said that Hitler had intentionally started the campaign against Russia at a time which would enable us to bring in the harvest. We thought that clever. On our endless journey we saw by the wayside dead Russians, burnt-out tanks, broken-down trucks, dead horses. And there were wounded Russians too lying there helpless, with nobody to care for them; all the way we could hear their screams and groans.

"One of my comrades spat at them and I protested. He simply replied with a phrase that our officer had used: 'No pity for Ivan . . .'

"His words sounded like a sober military command. He spoke in the style of a war correspondent. His words were parrot-like, unthinking. His conversation was full of stupid phrases which he had taken from newspapers.

"Finally we came to a Ukrainian village and here I had my first contact with the enemy. We shot up a deserted farmhouse in which Russians had barricaded themselves. When we stormed it we found only a few wounded men lying about with whom we did not bother. That is, I did not bother. But our platoon leader . . . Gave them the coup-de-grâce . . .

"Since I have been in hospital here these details constantly recur to me. I live it all over again, but much more precisely and vividly . . . Now I have plenty of time.

"The fighting was inhuman. Many of us could hardly stand it. When our major saw this he shouted to us: 'Believe you me, do you think the Russians act differently towards our men? You need only see how they treat their own people. The prisons we come across are full of murdered men. They simply mow down their prisoners when they cannot take them away. He who has been selected to make history cannot be bothered with such trifles.'

"One evening a comrade took me aside in order to express his horror, but after the very first sentence he stopped. He did not trust me.

"We continued to make history. Day after day we heard victory reports and constantly we were told that the war would soon be over. Hitler said so and Himmler . . . For me it is now really over . . ."

He took a deep breath. Then a sip of water. Behind me I heard a noise and looked round. I had not noticed that the door was open. But he had heard it.

"Sister, please . . ."

"All right, I only wanted to look round . . ."

She shut the door again.

"One hot summer day we came to Dnyepropetrovsk. Everywhere there were abandoned cars and guns. Many of them still intact. Obviously the Russians had left in great haste. Houses were burning and the streets were blocked by hastily erected barricades, but there was nobody left to defend them. There were deaths among the civilians. On the pavement I saw the body of a woman and over her crouched two weeping children . . .

"When the order came to fall out we leaned our rifles against the house walls, sat down and smoked. Suddenly we heard an explosion, and looked up, but there was no plane in sight. Then we saw a whole block of houses had blown up.

"Many house blocks had been mined by the Russians before they retreated and as soon as our troops entered, the buildings blew up. One comrade declared that the Russians had learnt such tactics from the Finns. I was glad we had been resting. We had escaped again.

"Suddenly a staff car stopped near us. A major climbed out and sent for our captain. Then came a number of trucks which took us to another part of the town. There the same miserable picture presented itself.

"In a large square we got out and looked around us. On the other side of the square there was a group of people under close guard. I assumed they were civilians who were to be taken out of the town, in which fighting was still going on. And then the word ran through our group like wildfire: 'They're Jews' . . . In my young life I had never seen many

Jews. No doubt there had formerly been some, but for the most part they had emigrated when Hitler came to power. The few who remained simply disappeared later. It was said they had been sent to the Ghetto. Then they were forgotten. My mother sometimes mentioned our family doctor, who was a Jew and for whom she mourned deeply. She carefully preserved all his prescriptions, for she had complete trust in his medical knowledge. But one day the chemist told her that she must get her medicines prescribed by a different doctor, he was not allowed to make up the prescriptions of a Jewish doctor. My mother was furious but my father just looked at me and held his tongue.

"I need not tell you what the newspapers said about the Jews. Later in Poland I saw Jews who were quite different from ours in Stuttgart. At the army base at Debicka some Jews were still working and I often gave them something to eat. But I stopped when the platoon leader caught me doing it. The Jews had to clean out our quarters and I often deliberately left behind on the table some food which I knew they would find.

"Otherwise all I knew about the Jews was what came out of the loudspeaker or what was given us to read. We were told they were the cause of all our misfortunes . . . They were trying to get on top of us, they were the cause of war, poverty, hunger, unemployment . . ."

I noticed that the dying man had a warm undertone in his voice as he spoke about the Jews. I had never heard such a tone in the voice of an SS man. Was he better than the others—or did the voices of SS men change when they were dying?

"An order was given," he continued, "and we marched towards the huddled mass of Jews. There were a hundred and fifty of them or perhaps two hundred, including many children who stared at us with anxious eyes. A few were quietly crying. There were infants in their mothers' arms, but hardly any young men; mostly women and greybeards.

"As we approached I could see the expression in their eyes—fear, indescribable fear . . . apparently they knew what was awaiting them . . .

"A truck arrived with cans of petrol which we unloaded and took into a house. The stronger men among the Jews were ordered to carry the cans to the upper storeys. They obeyed—apathetically, without a will of their own, like automatons.

"Then we began to drive the Jews into the house. A sergeant with a whip in his hand, helped any of the Jews who were not quick enough. There was a hail of curses and kicks. The house was not very large, it had only three storeys. I would not have believed it possible to crowd them all into it. But after a few minutes there was no Jew left on the street."

He was silent and my heart started to beat violently. I could well imagine the scene. It was all too familiar. I might have been among those who were forced into that house with the petrol cans. I could feel how they must have pressed against each other; I could hear their frantic cries as they realised what was to be done to them.

The dying Nazi went on: "Then another truck came up full of more Jews and they too were crammed into the house with the others. Then the door was locked and a machine-gun was posted opposite."

I knew how this story would end. My own country had been occupied by the Germans for over a year and we had heard of similar happenings in Bialystok, Brody and Grodek. The method was always the same. He could spare me the rest of his gruesome account.

So I stood up ready to leave but he pleaded with me: "Please stay. I must tell you the rest."

I really do not know what kept me. But there was something in his voice that prevented me from obeying my instinct to end the interview. Perhaps I wanted to hear from his own mouth, in his own words, the full horror of the Nazis' inhumanity.

"When we were told that everything was ready, we went back a few yards, and then received the command to remove safety pins from hand grenades and throw them through the windows of the house. Detonations followed one after another . . . My God!"

Now he was silent, and he raised himself slightly from the bed: his whole body was shivering.

But he continued: "We heard screams and saw the flames eat their way from floor to floor . . . We had our rifles ready to shoot down anyone who tried to escape from that blazing hell . . .

"The screams from the house were horrible. Dense smoke poured out and choked us . . ."

His hand felt damp. He was so shattered by his recollection that he broke into a sweat and I loosened my hand from his grip. But at once he groped for it again and held it tight.

"Please, please," he stammered, "don't go away, I have more to say."

I no longer had any doubts as to the ending. I saw that he was summoning his strength for one last effort to tell me the rest of the story to its bitter end.

". . . Behind the windows of the second floor, I saw a man with a small child in his arms. His clothes were alight. By his side stood a woman, doubtless the mother of the child. With his free hand the man covered the child's eyes—then he jumped into the street. Seconds later the mother followed.

Then from the other windows fell burning bodies ... We shot ... Oh God!"

The dying man held his hand in front of his bandaged eyes as if he wanted to banish the picture from his mind.

"I don't know how many tried to jump out of the windows but that one family I shall never forget—least of all the child. It had black hair and dark eyes ..."

He fell silent, completely exhausted.

The child with the dark eyes he had described reminded me of Eli, a boy from the Lemberg Ghetto, six years old with large, questioning eyes—eyes that could not understand—accusing eyes—eyes that one never forgets.

The children in the Ghetto grew up quickly, they seemed to realise how short their existence would be. For them days were months, and months were years. When I saw them with toys in their hands, they looked unfamiliar, uncanny, like old men playing with childish things.

When had I first seen Eli? When did I talk to him for the first time? I could not remember. He lived in a house near the Ghetto gate. Sometimes he wandered right up to the gate. On one occasion I heard a Jewish policeman talking to him and that is how I knew his name—Eli. It was rarely that a child dared to approach the Ghetto gate. Eli knew that. He knew it from instinct without understanding why.

"Eli" is a pet name for Elijah—Eljahu Hanavi, the prophet.

Recalling the very name awoke memories in me of the time when I too was a child. At the Passover Seder, there stood on the table among the dishes a large, ornate bowl of wine which nobody was allowed to touch. The wine was meant for Eljahu Hanavi. After a special prayer one of us children was sent to open the door: the Prophet was supposed to come into the room and drink the wine reserved for him. We children watched the door with eyes large with wonder. But, of course, nobody came. But my grandmother always assured me that the Prophet actually drank from the cup and when I looked into the cup and found that it was still full, she said: "He doesn't drink more than a tear!"

Why did she say that? Was a tear all that we could offer the Prophet Elijah? For countless generations since the exodus from Egypt we had been celebrating the Passover in its memory. And from that great event arose the custom of reserving a cup of wine for Eljahu Hanavi.

We children looked on Eljahu as our protector, and in our fancy he took every possible form. My grandmother told us that he was rarely recognisable; he might appear in the form of a village peasant, a shopkeeper, a beggar or even as a child. And in gratitude for the protection that he afforded us he was given the finest cup in the house at the Seder service filled with the best wine—but he drank no more than a single tear from it.

Little Eli in the Ghetto survived miraculously the many raids on the children, who were looked upon as "non-working, useless mouths". The adults worked all day outside the Ghetto, and it was during their absence that the SS usually rounded up the children and took them away. A few always escaped the body-snatchers for the children learnt how to hide themselves. Their parents built hiding holes under the floors, in the stoves or in cupboards with false walls, and in time they developed a sort of sixth sense for danger, no matter how small they were.

But gradually the SS discovered the cleverest hiding places and they came out the winners in this game of hide-and-seek with death.

Eli was one of the last children that I saw in the Ghetto.

Each time I left the camp for the Ghetto—for a period I had an entry permit for it—I looked for Eli. If I saw him I could be sure that for the moment there was no danger. There was already famine at that time in the Ghetto, and the streets were littered with people dying of hunger. The Jewish policemen constantly warned Eli's parents to keep him away from the gate, but in vain. The German policeman at the Ghetto gate often gave him something to eat.

One day when I entered the Ghetto Eli was not by the gate but I saw him later. He was standing by a window and his tiny hand was sweeping up something from the sill. Then his fingers went to his mouth. As I came closer I realised what he was doing, and my eyes filled with tears: he was collecting the crumbs which somebody had put out for the birds. No doubt he figured that the birds would find some nourishment outside the Ghetto, from friendly people in the city who dare not give a hungry Jewish child a piece of bread.

Outside the Ghetto gate there were often women with sacks of bread or flour trying to barter with the inmates of the Ghetto, food for clothes, silver plate or carpets. But there were few Jews left who possessed anything they could barter with.

Eli's parents certainly had nothing to offer in exchange for even a loaf of bread.

SS Group Leader Katzmann—the notorious Katzmann—knew that there must still be children in the Ghetto in spite of repeated searches so his brutish brain conceived a devilish plan: he would start a kindergarten! He told the Jewish Council that he would set up a kindergarten if they could find accommodation for it and a woman to run it. Then the children would be looked after while the grown-ups were out at work. The Jews, eternal and incorrigible optimists, took this as a sign of a more humane attitude. They even told each other that there was now a regulation against shooting. Somebody said that he had heard on the American radio that Roosevelt had threatened the Germans with reprisals if any more Jews were killed. That was why the Germans were going to be more humane in future.

Others talked of an International Commission which was going to visit the Ghetto. The Germans wanted to show them a kindergarten—as proof of their considerate treatment of the Jews.

An official from the Gestapo named Engels, a greyhaired man, came with a member of the Jewish Council to see for himself that the kindergarten was actually set up in suitable rooms. He said he was sure there were still enough children in the Ghetto who would like to use the kindergarten, and he promised an extra ration of food. And the Gestapo did actually send tins of cocoa and milk.

Thus the parents of the hungry children still left were gradually persuaded to send them to the kindergarten. A committee from the Red Cross was anxiously awaited. But it never came. Instead, one morning three SS trucks arrived and took all the children away to the gas chambers. And that night, when the parents came back from work, there were heart-rending scenes in the deserted kindergarten.

Nevertheless, a few weeks later I saw Eli again. His instinct had made him stay at home on that particular morning.

For me the dark-eyed child of whom the man in the bed had spoken was Eli. His little face would be stamped on my memory for ever. He was the last Jewish child that I had seen.

Up to this moment my feelings towards the dying man had tended towards sympathy: now all that was past. The touch of his hand caused me almost physical pain and I drew away.

But I still didn't think of leaving. There was something

more to come: of that I was sure. His story must go on . . .

He murmured something which I did not understand. My thoughts were far away, although I was here only to listen to what he was so anxious to tell me. It seemed to me that he was forgetting my presence, just as for a time I had forgotten his. He was talking to himself in a monotone. Sick people when they are alone often talk to themselves. Was he continuing the story that he wanted to tell me? Or was it something that he would like to tell me but which he dare not express in comprehensible words. Who knows what he still had to say? Unimaginable. One thing I had learnt: no deed was so awful that its wickedness could not be surpassed.

"Yes, I see them plain before my eyes . . ." he muttered.

What was he saying? How could he see them? His head and eyes were swathed in bandages.

"I can see the child and his father and his mother," he went on.

He groaned and his breath came gasping from his lungs.

"Perhaps they were already dead when they struck the pavement. It was frightful. Screams mixed with volleys of shots. The volleys were probably intended to drown the shrieks. I can never forget—it haunts me. I have had plenty of time to think, but yet perhaps not enough . . ."

Did I now hear shots? We were so used to shooting that nobody took any notice. But I could hear them quite plainly. There was constant shooting in the camp. I shut my eyes and in my memory I heard and saw all the shocking details.

During his narration, which often consisted of short, broken phrases, I could see and hear everything as clearly as if I had been there. I saw the wretches being driven into the house, I heard their screams, I heard them praying for their children and then I saw them leaping in flames to earth.

"Shortly afterwards we moved on. On the way we were

told that the massacre of the Jews was in revenge for the Russian time-bombs which had cost us about thirty men. We had killed three hundred Jews in exchange. Nobody asked what the murdered Jews had to do with the Russian time-bombs.

"In the evening there was a ration of brandy. Brandy helps one forget . . . Over the radio came reports from the front, the numbers of torpedoed ships, of prisoners taken, or planes shot down and the area of the newly-conquered territories . . . It was getting dark . . .

"Fired by the brandy we sat down and began to sing. I too sang. Today I ask myself how I could have done that. Perhaps I wanted to anaesthetise myself. For a time I was successful. The events seemed to recede further and further away. But during the night they came back . . .

"A comrade who slept next to me was Peter and he too came from Stuttgart. He was restless in his sleep, tossing to and fro and muttering. I sat up and stared at him. But it was too dark to see his face and I could only hear him saying, 'No, no', and 'I won't'. In the morning I could see by the faces of some of my comrades that they too had had a restless night. But nobody would talk about it. They avoided each other. Even our platoon leader noticed it.

" 'You and your sensitive feelings! Men, you cannot go on like this. This is war! One must be hard! They are not our people. The Jew is not a human being! The Jews are the cause of all our misfortunes! And when you shoot one of them it is not the same thing as shooting one of us—it doesn't matter whether it is man, woman or child, they are different from us. Without question one must get rid of them. If we had been soft we should still be other people's slaves, but the Führer . . .'

"Yes, you see," he began but did not continue.

What had he been going to say? Something perhaps that might be of comfort to himself. Something that might explain why he was telling me his life story? But he did not return to the subject.

"Our rest period did not last long. Towards midday we resumed the advance, we were now part of the storm troops. We mounted the trucks and were transported to the firing line, but here too there was not much to be seen of the enemy. He had evacuated villages and small towns, giving them up without a fight. There were only occasional skirmishes as the enemy retreated. Peter was wounded, Karlheinz killed. Then we had another rest, with time to wash up and to write letters. Talk centred on different subjects, but there was hardly a word said about the happenings in Dnyepropetrovsk.

"I went to see Peter. He had been shot in the abdomen but was still conscious. He recognised me and looked at me with tears in his eyes. I sat down by him and he told me he was soon to be taken away to hospital. He said, 'The people in that house, you know what I mean . . .' Then he lost consciousness. Poor Peter. He died with the memory of the most dreadful experience of his life."

I now heard footsteps in the corridor. I looked towards the door which might open at any moment, and stood up. He stopped me.

"Do stay, the nurse is waiting outside. Nobody will come in. I won't keep you much longer, but I still have something important to say . . ."

I sat down again unwillingly but made up my mind to depart as soon as the nurse returned.

What could this man still have to tell me? That he was not the only person who had murdered Jews, that he was simply a murderer among murderers?

He resumed his soulsearching: "In the following weeks we advanced towards the Crimea. Rumour had it that there was hard fighting in front of us, the Russians were well entrenched; it wasn't going to be a walk-over any more, but close fighting, man to man . . ."

He paused for breath. The pauses were becoming more frequent. Obviously he was overtaxing his strength. His breathing was irregular; his throat seemed to dry up: his hand groped for the glass of water.

I did not move. He appeared content as long as he was aware of my presence.

He found the glass and gulped down some water.

Then he sighed and whispered: "My God, my God."

Was he talking about God? But God was absent—on leave, as the woman in the Ghetto had said. Yet we all needed Him; we all longed to see signs of His omnipresence.

For this dying man, however, and for his like there could be no God. The Führer had taken His place. And the fact that their atrocities remained unpunished merely strengthened their belief that God was a fiction, a hateful Jewish invention. They never tired of trying to "prove" it. But now this man, who was dying here in his bed was asking for God!

He went on: "The fighting in the Crimea lasted for weeks. We had severe losses. Everywhere military cemeteries sprang up. I heard they were well tended and on every grave were growing flowers. I like flowers. There were many in my uncle's garden. I used to lie on the grass for hours and admire the flowers . . ."

Did he know already that he would get a sunflower when he was buried? The murderer would own something even when he was dead . . . And I?

"We were approaching Taganrog, which was strongly held by Russians. We lay among the hills, barely a hundred yards from them. Their artillery fire was incessant. We cowered in our trenches and tried to conquer our fear by drinking from brandy flasks passed from hand to hand. We waited for the order to attack. It came at last and we climbed out of the trenches and charged, but suddenly I stopped as though rooted to the ground. Something seized me. My hands, which held my rifle with fixed bayonet, began to tremble.

"In that moment I saw the burning family, the father with the child and behind them the mother—and they came to meet me. 'No, I cannot shoot at them a second time.' The thought flashed through my mind ... And then a shell exploded by my side. I lost consciousness.

"When I woke in hospital I knew that I had lost my eyesight. My face and the upper part of my body were torn to ribbons. The nurse told me that the surgeon had taken a whole basinful of shell splinters out of my body. It was a miracle that I was still alive—even now I am as good as dead ..."

He sighed. His thoughts were once again centred on himself and he was filled with self-pity.

"The pain became more and more unbearable. My whole body is covered with marks from pain-killing injections ... I was taken from one field hospital to another, but they never sent me home ... That was the real punishment for me. I wanted to go home to my mother. I knew what my father would say in his inflexible severity. But my mother ... She would look at me with other eyes."

I saw that he was torturing himself. He was determined to gloss over nothing.

Once again he groped for my hand, but I had withdrawn it sometime before and was sitting on it, out of his reach. I did not want to be touched by the hand of death. He sought my pity, but had he any right to pity? Did a man of his kind deserve anybody's pity? Did he think he would find pity if he pitied himself ...

"Look," he said, "those Jews died quickly, they did not suffer as I do—though they were not as guilty as I am."

At this I stood up to go—I, the last Jew in his life. But he held me fast with his white, bloodless hand. Whence could a man drained of blood derive such strength?

"I was taken from one hospital to another, they never sent me home. But I told you that before . . . I am well aware of my condition and all the time I have been lying here I have never stopped thinking of the horrible deed at Dnyepropetrovsk. If only I had not survived that shell—but I can't die yet, although I have often longed to die . . . Sometimes I hoped that the doctor would give me an injection to put me out of my misery. I have indeed asked him to put me to sleep. But he has no pity for me although I know he has released other dying men from their sufferings by means of injections. Perhaps he is deterred by my youth. On the board at the foot of my bed is not only my name but also my date of birth, perhaps that keeps him back. So I lie here waiting for death. The pains in my body are terrible, but worse still is my conscience. It never ceases to remind me of the burning house and the family that jumped from the window."

He lapsed into silence, seeking for words. He wants something from me, I thought, for I could not imagine that he had brought me here merely as an audience.

"When I was still a boy I believed with my mind and soul in God and in the commandments of the Church. Then everything was easier. If I still had that faith I am sure death would not be so hard.

"I cannot die. . . without coming clean. This must be my confession. But what sort of confession is this? A letter without an answer . . ."

No doubt he was referring to my silence. But what could I say? Here was a dying man—a murderer who did not want to be a murderer but who had been made into a murderer by a murderous ideology. He was confessing his crime to a man who perhaps tomorrow must die at the hands of these same murderers. In his confession there was true repentance, even though he did not admit it in so many words. Nor was it necessary, for the way in which he spoke and the fact that he spoke to *me* was a proof of his repentance.

"Believe me, I would be ready to suffer worse and longer pains if by that means I could bring back the dead, at Dnyepropetrovsk. Many young Germans of my age die daily on the battlefields. They have fought against an armed enemy and have fallen in the fight, but I . . . I am left here with my guilt. In the last hours of my life you are with me. I do not know who you are, I only know that you are a Jew and that is enough."

I said nothing. The truth was that on his battlefield he had also "fought" against defenceless men, women, children and the aged. I could imagine them enveloped in flames jumping from the windows to certain death.

He sat up and put his hands together as if to pray.

"I want to die in peace, and so I need . . ."

I saw that he could not get the words past his lips. But I was in no mood to help him. I kept silent.

"I know that what I have told you is terrible. In the long nights while I have been waiting for death, time and time again I have longed to talk about it to a Jew and beg forgiveness from him. Only I didn't know whether there were any Jews left . . .

"I know that what I am asking is almost too much for you, but without your answer I cannot die in peace."

Now, there was an uncanny silence in the room. I looked through the window. The front of the buildings opposite was flooded with sunshine. The sun was high in the heavens. There was only a small triangular shadow in the courtyard.

What a contrast between the glorious sunshine outside and the shadow of this bestial age here in the death chamber! Here lay a man in bed who wished to die in peace—but he could not, because of the memory of his terrible crime gave him no rest. And by him sat a man also doomed to die—but who did not want to die because he yearned to see the end of all the horror that blighted the world.

Two men who had never known each other had been brought together for a few hours by Fate. One asks the other for help. But the other was himself helpless and able to do nothing for him.

I stood up and looked in his direction, at his folded hands. Between them there seemed to rest a sunflower.

At last I made up my mind and without a word I left the room.

The nurse was not outside the door. I forgot where I was and did not go back down the staircase up which the nurse had brought me. As I used to do in student days, I went downstairs to the main entrance and it was not until I saw surprised looks from the nurses and doctors that I realised I was taking the wrong way down. But I did not retreat. Nobody stopped me and I walked through the main door into the open air and returned to my comrades . . . The sun at its zenith was blazing down.

My comrades were sitting on the grass spooning soup out of their mess tins. I too was hungry, and just in time to get the last of the soup. The hospital had made us all a present of a meal.

But my thoughts were still with the dying SS man. The

encounter with him was a heavy burden on me, his confession had profoundly disturbed me.

"Where have you been all this time?" asked somebody. I did not know his name. He had been marching beside me the whole way from the camp to the hospital.

"I was beginning to think you had made a bolt for it which would have meant a nice reception for us back in the camp."

I did not reply.

"Did you get anything?" he asked as he peered into the empty bread sack, which, like every other prisoner I carried over my shoulder. He looked at me suspiciously, as to imply: you've got something, but won't admit it for fear of having to share it with us.

I let him think what he liked and said nothing.

"Are you annoyed with me?" he questioned.

"No," said I. I didn't want to talk to him—not at that moment.

After a short pause we resumed work. There seemed to be no end to the containers which we had to empty. The trucks which carried the rubbish to be burnt somewhere in the open kept coming back incessantly. Where did they take all this refuse? But really I did not care. The only thing I desired was to get away from this place.

At long last we were told to stop work, and to come back the next day to cart away more rubbish. I went cold when I heard this.

On the way back to the camp our guards, the askaris, didn't seem to be in a singing mood. They marched along beside us in silence and did not even urge us on. We were all tired, even I, who had spent most of the day in a sick room. Had it really lasted several hours? Again and again my thoughts returned to that macabre encounter.

On the footpaths, past which we were marching, people

were staring at us. I could not distinguish one face from another, they all seemed to be exactly alike—probably because they were all so utterly indifferent to us in spite of their stares.

Anyhow, why should they behave otherwise? They were long since used to the sight of us. Of what concern were we to them? A few might later on suffer the pangs of conscience for gawking at doomed men so callously.

We were not walking fast, because a horse and cart in front impeded us. I had time to conjecture that among these people must be many who had once been amused at the "day without the Jews" in the High School, and I asked myself if it was only the Nazis who had persecuted us. Was it not just as wicked for people to look on quietly and without protest at human beings enduring such shocking humiliation? But in their eyes were we human beings at all?

Two days before, some newcomers at the camp had told us a very sad but also a very characteristic story. Three Jews had been hanged in public. They were left swinging on the gallows, and a witty fellow had fastened to each body a piece of paper bearing the words "kosher meat". The bystanders had split their sides with laughter at this brilliant joke, and there was a constant stream of spectators to share in the merriment. A woman who disapproved of the vile obscenity was promptly beaten up.

We all knew that at public executions the Nazis were at pains to encourage large audiences. They hoped thus to terrify the populace and so stifle any further resistance. Of course they were well aware of the anti-Jewish feeling of most onlookers. These executions corresponded to the "bread and circuses" of ancient Rome, and the ghastly scenes staged by the Nazis were by no means generally resented. All of us in camp were tireless in describing every detail of the horrors we had witnessed. Some talked as if they had just got home after a circus performance. Perhaps some of those who were now standing on the pavement and gaping at us were people who would gape at gibbeted Jews. I heard laughter—perhaps the show they were witnessing, a march past of kosher meat, tickled their fancy.

At the end of Grodezka Street we turned left into Janowska Street and we were brought to a halt to let a string of crowded tramcars go past. People clung to the doors like bunches of grapes, tired but happy people struggling to get home to their families, where they would spend the evening together, playing cards, discussing politics, listening to the radio—perhaps even listening to forbidden foreign transmissions. They all had one thing in common: they had dreams and hopes. We, on the other hand, had to attend the evening roll-call and perform gymnastic exercises laid down according to the mood of the officer in charge. Often doing interminable knee bends until the officer tired of his joke. Or there awaited us the "vitamin B" exercise in which hour after hour we had to carry planks through a lane of SS men. Evening work was dubbed "vitamins", but unlike the real vitamins, these killed not cured.

If a man was missing at roll-call, they would count us over and over again, and then in place of the missing man they would take any ten of his comrades out of the ranks and execute them as a deterrent to other would-be absentees.

And the same thing would happen tomorrow, and perhaps the day after tomorrow, until we were all gone.

Thoughts of tomorrow ... made me think of the dying SS man with his bandaged head. Tomorrow or perhaps the day after tomorrow he would get his sunflower. For me, tomorrow or the day after tomorrow, perhaps a mass grave waited. Indeed at any moment the order might come to clear

61

the hut in which I and my comrades slept—or I might be one of the ten to be selected as a deterrent.

One day a rumour ran round the camp that fresh prisoners were arriving from the provinces. If so, there would be no room in our existing huts, and if the camp authorities couldn't raise any new ones, they would make room in another way. Quite a simple matter, they simply liquidated the original prisoners—hut by hut, to make room for the newcomers. It happened every two months. It accelerated the natural decrease in our numbers, and the goal of making Galicia and Lemberg "Jew-free", grew ever nearer.

The narrow-fronted houses in Janowska Street were a dirty grey and showed traces of war damage: bullet marks on the house fronts and windows boarded up, sometimes merely with cardboard. Janowska Street was one of the most important arteries in Lemberg, and violent fighting had taken place there when the Germans had captured the city.

At the end of the rows of houses we passed once again the military cemetery with its long lines of graves, but somehow the sunflowers looked different now. They were facing in another direction. The evening sunshine gave them a reddish tinge, and they trembled gently in the breeze. They seemed to be whispering to each other. Were they horrified by the ragged men who were marching past on tired feet? The colours of the sunflowers—orange and yellow, gold and brown—danced before my eyes. They grew in a fertile brown soil, from carefully tended mounds—and behind them grew gnarled trees forming a dark background, and above everything hovered the deep-blue clear sky.

As we neared camp, the askaris gave the order to sing, and to march in step and proper formation. The commandant might be watching the return of his prisoners and he insisted they must always march out singing and (apparently) happy, and return in the same way. The askaris had to help him to keep up the pretence. We must radiate contentment—and singing was part of it.

Woe to us if our performance did not satisfy the commandant! We suffered for it. The askaris too would have nothing to laugh at—after all they were only Russians.

Luckily the commandant was nowhere to be seen so we marched into camp behind another working party unobserved and fell in on the parade ground for roll-call.

I saw Arthur in another column and waved to him furtively. I was dying to tell him about my experience in the hospital, and also to tell Josek.

I wondered what these two men so different from each other would have to say. I also wanted to talk to them about the sunflowers. Why had we never noticed them before? They had been in flower for weeks. Had nobody noticed them? Or was I the only person for whom they had any significance?

We were lucky, roll-call was over sooner than usual and I touched Arthur on the shoulder.

"Well, how was it? Hard work?" He smiled at me in a friendly way.

"Not so bad. Do you know where I was?"

"No. How should I know?"

"At the Technical High School."

"Really? But in a different capacity than formerly!"

"You may well say that."

"You look rather depressed," Arthur remarked.

I did not reply. The men were crowding towards the kitchen and soon we were standing in a queue waiting for the food issue.

Josek came past us with his mess tin full. He nodded to us. We sat on the steps in front of the hut door eating our food and on the parade ground stood groups of prisoners telling each other of the day's happenings. Some of them perhaps had succeeded in scrounging oddments during their work outside the camp and they were now exchanging these among each other.

My gaze wandered to the "pipe", a narrow, fenced passage running round the inner camp and ending at the sandhills where the executions usually took place.

Sometimes men waited for two or three days in the "pipe" before they were murdered. The SS fetched them out of the huts or arrested them in the city, where they had been in hiding. They operated a "rational" system of shooting a number of men together, so several days would sometimes pass before the number was large enough to warrant the SS executioner's effort to make his way to the sandhills.

On that particular evening there was nothing to be seen in the "pipe". Arthur told me why. "There were five today but they had not long to wait. Kauzor fetched them. A fellow in our hut knew them and said they had been unearthed in a good hiding place in the city."

Arthur spoke calmly and quietly as if he was recounting something very commonplace.

"There was a boy among them," he continued after a while, and now his voice was a little more emotional. "He had lovely fair hair. He didn't look the slightest bit Jewish. If his parents had put him into an Aryan family, he would never have been noticed."

I thought of Eli.

"Arthur, I must talk to you. In the High School, which they are now using as a military hospital, I had an experience today which I am not finished with. You might laugh at me when you hear it, but I want to know just what you think about it. I have faith in your judgment."

"Go on," he said.

"No, not now. We will talk about it later. I want Josek to be there to hear it."

Was I right after all to tell them what had happened? I thought of the five men in the "pipe" who had been shot that day. Was this SS man more to me than they were? Perhaps it was better to keep my mouth shut about what I had heard in the hospital death chamber.

I feared that Arthur, the cynic, might say: "Just look at him; he can't forget a dying SS man while countless Jews are tortured and killed every hour." He might add: "You have let yourself be infected by the Nazis. You are beginning to think that the Germans are in some way superior, and that's why you are worrying about your dying SS man."

This would hurt me and then no doubt Arthur would tell me about the unspeakable crimes that the Nazis had committed. I would be ashamed of myself. So perhaps it was better to keep to myself what had happened in the hospital.

I strolled over to the parade ground and chatted to some acquaintances.

Suddenly one of them hissed: "Six!" That was the agreed warning that SS men were approaching. I hurried back to Arthur and sat down by him as the two SS men walked to the bandsmen's hut.

"What were you going to tell us?" asked Arthur.

"I have been thinking it over and I don't want to talk about it. You might not understand or . . ."

"Or what? Tell us," Arthur insisted.

I was silent.

"All right, as you like." Arthur stood up. He seemed annoyed.

But two hours later I told them the story. We were sitting in our stuffy hut on our bunks. I told them about our march through the city and about the sunflowers.

"Have either of you ever noticed them?"

"Of course I have," said Josek. "What is so special about them?"

I was reluctant to tell him the impression the sunflowers had made on me. I could not say I had envied the dead Germans their sunflowers or that I had been seized with a childish longing to have a sunflower of my own.

Arthur joined in: "Well, sunflowers are something to please the eye. The Germans after all are great romantics. But flowers aren't much use to those rotting under the earth. The sunflowers will rot away like them; next year there won't be a trace unless someone plants new ones. But who knows what's going to happen next year?" he added scornfully.

I continued my story. I described how the nurse had fetched me and taken me to the Dean's room, and then I told them in detail of the dying SS man by whose bed I had sat for hours, and of his confession. To the child who had leapt to death with his father I gave the name of Eli.

"How did the man know the child's name?" asked one of them.

"He didn't. I gave him the name because it reminded me of a boy in the Lemberg Ghetto."

They all seemed grimly fascinated by my story and once when I paused to gather my thoughts they urged me to go on.

When I finally described how the dying man had pleaded with me to pardon his crime and how I had left him without saying a word, I noticed a slight smile appear on Josek's face. I was sure it signified his agreement with my action and I nodded to him.

It was Arthur who first broke the silence: "One less!" he exclaimed.

The two words expressed exactly what we all felt in those days but Arthur's reaction somehow disturbed me. One of the men, Adam—he seldom wasted words—said thoughtfully: "So you saw a murderer dying . . . I would like to do that ten times a day. I couldn't have enough such hospital visits."

I understood his cynicism. Adam had studied architecture, but had had to abandon his career when the war broke out. During the Russian occupation he worked on building sites. All his family possessions had been nationalised by the Russians. When in the summer of 1940 the great wave of deportations to Siberia began, embracing all of "bad social origin" (i.e. especially members of the well-to-do classes) he and his family had hidden for weeks.

At our first meeting after his arrival in the camp he had said: "You see it was worthwhile hiding from the Russians. If they had caught me I should now be in Siberia. As it is I am still in Lemberg. Whether this may be an advantage . . ."

He was completely indifferent to his surroundings. His fiancée was in the Ghetto but he rarely had news from her. She must have been working in some army formation.

His parents to whom he was deeply devoted had perished in the very first days after the German occupation. Sometimes in his disregard for his surroundings he seemed to me like a sleepwalker. He grew more and more remote, and at first we could not rightly understand why. But gradually we all came to resemble him. We too had lost most of our relatives.

My story had apparently roused Arthur a little from his apathy, but for a long time nothing more was said by any of my listeners.

Then Arthur got up and went to a bunk where a friend of his was retailing the radio news. And the others went about their own business.

Only Josek stayed with me.

"Do you know," he began, "when you were telling us about your meeting with the SS man, I feared at first, that you had really forgiven him. You would have had no right to do this in the name of people who had not authorised you to do so. What people have done to you yourself, you can, if you like, forgive and forget. That is your own affair. But it would have been a terrible sin to burden your conscience with other people's sufferings."

"But aren't we a single community with the same destiny, and one must answer for the other," I interrupted.

"Be careful, my friend," continued Josek. "In each person's life there are historic moments which rarely occur—and today you have experienced one such. It is not a simple problem for you ... I can see you are not entirely pleased with yourself. But I assure you that I would have done the same as you did. The only difference perhaps is that I would have refused my pardon quite deliberately and openly and yet with a clear conscience. You acted more unconsciously. And now you don't know whether it was right or wrong. But believe me it was right. You have suffered nothing because of him, and it follows that what he has done to other people you are in no position to forgive."

Josek's face was transfigured.

"I believe in Haolam Emes—in life after death, in another, better world, where we will all meet again after we are dead. How would it seem then if you had forgiven him? Would not the dead people from Dnyepropetrovsk come to you and ask: 'Who gave you the right to forgive our murderer?' "

I shook my head thoughtfully. "Josek," I said, "you make it all sound so simple, probably because your faith is strong. I could argue with you for hours, although I would not want to alter my actions—even if I could. I will only say one thing, and I am anxious to know what you think: the fellow showed a deep and genuine repentance, he did not once try to excuse what he had done. I saw that he was really in torment ...''

Josek interrupted: "Such torment is only a small part of his punishment."

"But," I continued, "he has no time left to repent or atone for his crimes."

"What do you mean by 'atone for'?"

He now had me where he wanted me: I had no reply. I dropped the argument and tried another gambit.

"This dying man looked on me as a representative, as a symbol of the other Jews whom he could no longer reach or talk to. And moreover he showed his repentance entirely of his own accord. Obviously he was not born a murderer nor did he want to be a murderer. It was the Nazis who made him kill defenceless people."

"So you mean you ought to have forgiven him after all?"

At this juncture Arthur came back. He had heard only Josek's last sentence and in his quiet voice he said: "A superman has asked a sub-human to do something which is superhuman. If you had forgiven him, you would never have forgiven yourself all your life."

"Arthur," I said, "I have failed to carry out the last wish of a dying man. I gave him no answer to his final question!"

"But surely you must know there are requests that one cannot and dare not grant. He ought to have sent for a priest of his own Church. They would soon have come to an agreement."

Arthur's words were delicately, almost imperceptibly ironical.

"Why," I asked, "is there then no general law of guilt and expiation? Has every religion its own ethics, its own answers?"

"Probably, yes."

There was nothing more to say. What in those circumstances, in those terrible times, could be said, had been said. The subject dropped.

To distract our thoughts, Arthur told us about the news that he had heard but his words met with only half my attention.

In thought I was still in the death chamber of the German hospital.

Perhaps Arthur was wrong. Perhaps his idea of the superman asking a sub-human for something superhuman was not more than a phrase which sounded very enlightened, but was no real answer. The SS man's attitude towards me was not that of an arrogant superman. Probably I hadn't successfully conveyed all my feelings: a sub-human condemned to death at the bedside of an SS man condemned to death . . . Perhaps I hadn't communicated the atmosphere and the despair at his crime so clearly expressed in his words.

And suddenly I was assailed by a doubt as to the reality of all this. Had I actually been in the Dean's room that day?

It all seemed to me doubtful, as doubtful and unreal as our whole existence in those days . . . it could not have been all true; it was a dream induced by hunger and despair . . . it was too illogical—like the whole of our lives.

The prisoner in the camp was driven, and he had to learn to let himself be driven without a will of his own. In our world, nothing any longer obeyed the laws of normal everyday life, here everything had its own logic. What laws were still valid in captivity? The only law that was left as a reliable basis for judgment was the law of death. That law alone was logical, certain and irrefutable. All other laws paled into insignificance, the result was a general passivity. We constantly reminded ourselves that this was the one law that was inevitable, that one could do nothing to change it. The effect on us was a mental paralysis, and the inconsolable attitude in which we were enveloped was the clear expression of the hopelessness of our lot.

During the night I saw Eli. His face seemed paler than ever and his eyes expressed the dumb, eternally unanswered question: Why?

His father brought him to me in his arms. As he approached he covered his eyes with his hands. Behind the two figures raged a sea of flames from which they were fleeing. I wanted to take Eli, but all that existed was a bloody mess . . .

"What are you shouting about? You will bring the guards in."

Arthur shook me by the shoulders. I could see his face by the weak light bulb high above on the ceiling.

I was not yet fully awake. Before my eyes danced something resembling a bandaged head with yellow stains. Was that too a dream? I saw everything as if through frosted glass.

"I will bring you a glass of water; perhaps you are feverish," said Arthur as he shook me again. And then I looked him full in the face.

"Arthur," I stammered, "Arthur, I don't want to go on that working party to the hospital tomorrow."

"First of all," he replied "it is already today, and secondly you could perhaps get attached to another party. I will go to the hospital in your place."

Arthur was trying to calm me. He talked as if I were a child.

"Are you suddenly frightened to look death in the eye, just because you have seen an SS man dying? How many Jews have you seen killed; did that make you shout out in the night? Death is our constant companion, have you forgotten that? It doesn't even spare the SS."

"You had just gone to sleep when the guards came in and fetched one of us away—the man sleeping right at the back in the corner. They took him only as far as the door of the hut, and then he collapsed. He was dead. Wake up properly and come with me. Look at him and then you will understand that you are making too much fuss about your SS man."

Why did Arthur stress "your SS man"? Did he mean to hurt me?

He noticed the way I flinched. "Fine feelings nowadays are a luxury we can't afford. Neither you nor I."

"Arthur," I repeated, "I don't want to go back to the hospital."

"If they send you there, you'll have to go: there's nothing you can do. Many will be only too pleased not to stay in the camp all day." Arthur still seemed unable to understand me.

"I haven't told you about the people in the streets. I don't want to see any of them any more. And they mustn't see me either. I don't want their sympathy."

Arthur gave up. He turned round in his bunk and went to sleep. I tried to keep awake. I feared the dream would return. But then I suddenly saw the men in the street. And I realised that the break with the world around us was now complete. They did not like us Jews—and that was no new thing. Our fathers had crept out of the confines of the Ghetto into the open world. They had worked hard and done all they could to be recognised by their fellow creatures. But it was all in vain. If the Jews shut themselves away from the rest of the world they were foreign bodies. If they left their own world and conformed, then they were undesirable immigrants to be hated and rejected. Even in my youth I realised that I had been born a second-class citizen.

A wise man once said that the Jews were the salt of the earth. But the Poles thought that their land had been ruined by over-salting. Compared with Jews in other countries, therefore, we were perhaps better prepared for what the Nazis had in store for us. And perhaps we were thereby made more resistent.

From birth onwards we had lived with the Poles, grown up with them, gone to school with them, but nevertheless to them we were always foreigners. A bridge of mutual understanding between a Jew and a non-Jew was a rarity. And nothing had changed in that respect, even though the Poles were now themselves subjugated. Even in our common misery there were still barriers between us.

I no longer wanted even to look at Poles; in spite of everything, I preferred to stay in camp.

Next morning we assembled again for roll-call. I was hoping that Arthur would accompany me if I had to go back to the hospital, and if the nurse came to fetch me again I would ask her to take Arthur in my place.

The Commandant arrived. He was not always present at the roll-call; yesterday, for instance, he had not been there. He brought with him a large black dobermann on a lead. By him stood the officer (who was calling the roll) and other SS men.

First of all the prisoners were counted. Luckily the figure was correct.

Then the Commandant ordered: "Working parties fall in: as yesterday."

There was considerable confusion. The prisoners were supposed to fall in according to huts, not working parties. The rearrangement into working parties was not quick enough for the Commandant. He began to bellow.

The dog became restless and strained on its lead. Any moment the Commandant would let it loose. But again we were lucky. An officer came over from the Commandant's office with a message. Whatever it was he marched off with the dog, which saved us the usual gruesome scenes, and the aftermath of wounded and perhaps a few dead.

The band at the inner gate played a lively march as we moved off. SS men watched our ranks intently. From time to time they made a man fall out because he was conspicuous in some way or other. Perhaps he was not in step. Or perhaps he looked weaker than the others. He was then sent to the "pipe".

We were escorted by the same askaris as on the previous day. An SS man from the guard room placed himself at the head of our column. On the way I wondered where I could hide if the nurse came to look for me.

The cemetery with the sunflowers came into view again on our left. Soon the dying SS man in the hospital would join his comrades there. I tried to picture the spot reserved for him.

Yesterday my comrades had stared at the sunflowers as if spellbound, but today they seemed to disregard them. Only a few glanced at them. But my gaze traversed row after row, and I nearly stumbled over the heels of the man in front of me.

In Grodeska Street children were playing unconcernedly. They at least did not need to hide when a man in uniform appeared. How lucky they were.

My neighbour drew my attention to a passer-by.

"Do you see that fellow with the Tyrolean hat? The one with the feather."

"Certainly a German," said I.

"Sort of. He is now a racial German, but three years ago he was a fanatical Pole. I know him well. I lived near him. When the Jewish shops were looted, he was there, and when they beat up the Jews in the University he was there too. Moreover

74

he is sure to have volunteered when the Russians were looking for collaborators. He is the type who is always on the side
of the people in power. Probably he has raked up a German
ancestor from somewhere or other. But I am prepared to bet
that he could not speak a word of German until a short time
ago. The Nazis need people like him. They would be helpless
without them."

In fact one constantly heard of ethnic Germans striving to
make themselves one hundred and fifty per cent German. On
working parties one had to be careful to avoid them. They
were always anxious to prove they were earning their special
ration cards. Many of them tried to cover their imperfect
knowledge of German by being particularly beastly to Poles
and Jews. The existence of Poles and Jews to be victimised was
very welcome to them.

When we entered the courtyard of the Technical High
School, the askaris at once lay down on the grass and rolled
their fat cigarettes. Two lorries were already waiting for us
prisoners. The refuse containers were again full to overflow-
ing. There were shovels against a wall and each of us took one.

I tried to get a job on the trucks where the nurse would be
unlikely to find me. But an orderly had already chosen four
other men for the job.

Then I saw the nurse walking from one prisoner to another,
glancing at each of them. Was it going to be a repetition of
yesterday? Had the dying Nazi forgotten something? Suddenly she was standing in front of me.

"Please," she said, "come with me."

"I have to go on working here," I protested.

She turned to the orderly who was in charge of us and said
a few words to him. Then she pointed to me and came back.

"Put down your shovel," she said curtly, "and come with
me."

I followed her with fear in my heart. I could not bear to listen to another confession. It was beyond my powers. Most of all I feared that the dying man would renew his plea for forgiveness. Perhaps this time I would be weak enough to give in and so finish with the painful business.

But to my surprise the nurse took a different route from yesterday's. I had no idea where she was taking me. Perhaps to the mortuary? She searched among a bunch of keys and unlocked a door. We entered a room which looked as if it were used for storage. On wooden stands which stretched nearly to the ceiling, bundles and boxes were piled.

"Wait here," she ordered, "I will be back in a moment."

I stood still.

After a few moments she came back. In her hand she had a bundle tied up in a green ground sheet. Sewn to it was a piece of linen with an address.

Somebody passed along in the corridor. She looked around nervously and drew me into the storeroom. Then she gazed at me searchingly and said: "The man with whom you spoke yesterday died in the night. I had to promise to give you all his possessions. Except for his confirmation watch, which I am to send to his mother."

"I don't want anything, Sister. Send the lot to his mother."

Without a word she thrust the bundle at me but I refused to touch it.

"Please send it all to his mother, the address is on it."

The nurse looked at me uncertainly. I turned away and left her there. She did not try to hold me back. Apparently she had no inkling of what the SS man had told me on the previous day.

I went back to work in the courtyard. A hearse drove past. Were they taking away the SS man already?

"Hi you over there, you're asleep," shouted the orderly.

An askari heard him and came over flourishing a whip. In his eyes there was a sadistic gleam. But the orderly sent him away.

This time our midday meal was not provided by the hospital. The ordinary prisoners' food was brought to us from the camp—an evil-smelling, grey brew misnamed soup. We swallowed it ravenously. Soldiers stood around watching us as if we were animals being fed.

For the rest of the day I worked in a trance. When I was back again on the parade ground in the evening I could hardly remember the return march. I had not even glanced at the sunflowers.

Later I told my friends about the death of the SS man, but they were not interested. The whole incident was closed in their minds after the tale I had told them the day before. But they all agreed with me that I had done well to refuse the dead man's possessions. Josek said: "In the story you told us yesterday there were points that seemed to need further thought. I should have liked to discuss them with Rab Schloms, but he alas is no more. He could easily have proved to you that you acted rightly . . . But even so I am afraid that you will continue to worry about this business. But don't cudgel your brains over it. You had no right to forgive him, you could not forgive him, and it was quite right not to accept his things."

After a while he added: "The Talmud tells us . . ."

Arthur lost something of his otherwise unshakable self-possession. He said to Josek, "Don't make him any madder; he is already dreaming about it and shouting out in his sleep. Next time it may bring us misfortune. It only needs one of the guards to hear him shouting and he will put a bullet through him. It's happened before.

"And you," said Arthur, turning to me, "do stop talking about it. All this moaning and groaning leads to nothing. If we survive this camp—and I don't think we will—and if the world comes to its senses again, inhabited by people who look on each other as human beings, then there will be plenty of time to discuss the question of forgiveness. There will be votes for and against, there will be people who will never forgive you for not forgiving him ... But anyhow nobody who has not had our experience will be able to understand fully. When we here argue about the problem, we are indulging in a luxury which we in our position simply cannot afford."

Arthur was right, I could see that. That night I slept soundly without dreaming of Eli.

At the morning roll-call the inspector from the Eastern Railway was waiting for us. We could return to our former work.

Over two years passed. Years filled with suffering and constant spectre of death. Once I myself was about to be shot but I was saved by a miracle. And so I know the thoughts which a man has in the moments before death.

Arthur was no longer alive. He died in my arms during an epidemic of typhus. I held him fast as he lay in the death struggle and I wiped the foam from his lips with a cloth. In his last hours fever made him unconscious, mercifully for him.

Then one day Adam sprained his ankle at work. As he was marching out with his working party, the guard noticed he was limping. He was sent off at once to the "pipe", and there he waited two days before he and others were shot.

Josek too is dead. But I only heard about this much later. Our group had been posted to the Eastern Railway and quartered there, and one day some extra labour was sent over from the camp. Among them was Josek. I could look after him a bit now. We had some contact with the outside world and we got more food. I begged our "head Jew" to arrange for Josek to stay with us, but it was almost impossible to arrange that for an individual. We tried to persuade one of the overseers to ask for more permanent labour on the railway. But that too failed.

Then one day the extra labour from the camp came without Josek. He was ill and had been put on a working party within the camp. He had a high temperature, and from time to time when his strength failed him he had to rest. His comrades warned him when the SS man was approaching, but Josek was too weak even to stand up. He was finished off with a bullet—as punishment for being "work-shy".

Of all the men whom I knew in those years, hardly one was still alive. My time had apparently not yet come or death did not want me.

When the Germans withdrew before the advancing Red Army, the camp was evacuated and a column of prisoners and SS guards moved westwards to other camps. I went through the terrors of Plaszow; I got to know Gross-Rosen and Buchenwald, and finally after countless detours via auxiliary camps I landed at Mauthausen.

I was allocated straight away to Block 6, the death block. Although the gas chamber was working at full pressure, it could not keep up with the enormous number of candidates. Day and night above the crematoria there hung a great cloud of smoke, evidence that the death industry was in full swing.

It was unnecessary to hasten the "natural" process of death. Why provide so many corpses in so many batches? Undernourishment, exhaustion and diseases which were often harmless in themselves but which nevertheless carried off the weaker prisoners, could provide a slower and steadier, but just as certain stream of corpses for the crematoria.

We prisoners in Block 6 no longer had to work. And we

hardly saw any SS men, only the dead bodies, which were carried away at regular intervals by those comrades who still had a little strength left. And we saw the newcomers who took their places.

Our hunger was almost unbearable: we were given practically nothing to eat. Each day when we were allowed a short time outside the huts we threw ourselves on the ground tore up the scanty grass and ate it like cattle. After such "outings" the corpse carriers had their hands full, for few could digest this "food". The corpses were piled on to the handcarts, which formed an endless procession.

In this camp I had time for thought. It was obvious that the Germans were nearing their end. But so were we. The well-oiled machinery of murder was now running by itself, liquidating the last witnesses of the unspeakable crimes. I already surmised what was later to be confirmed: there were complete plans in existence for our final destruction as soon as the Americans approached the camp.

"Only another half hour till freedom, but only a quarter of an hour till death," as one of us said.

I lay on my bunk, wasted away to a skeleton. I looked at everything as through a thin curtain, which, I supposed, was the effect of hunger. Then I would fall into a restless doze. One night when I was neither awake nor asleep the SS man from the Lemberg Hospital reappeared to me. I had forgotten all about him, there were more important things and in any case hunger dulled the thinking processes. I realised that I only had a few days to live, or at best a few weeks and yet I remembered the SS man again and his confession. His eyes were no longer completely hidden; they looked at me through small holes in the bandages. There was an angry expression in them. He was holding something in front of me—the bundle that I had refused to accept from the nurse. I must have screamed. A doctor, a young Jew from Cracow with whom I had sometimes conversed was on watch that night.

To this day I do not know why there was a doctor in Block 6. He couldn't help us, for his whole stock of drugs consisted of indefinable red pastilles and a little paper wadding. But this was enough for the authorities to pretend that there was a physician to look after the 1,500 condemned men in Block 6.

"What's the matter with you?" asked the doctor whom I found standing by my bunk. Four of us had to sleep on a single bunk and naturally the other three had been roused.

"What's the matter?" he repeated.

"I was only dreaming."

"Dreaming? I only wish I were able to dream again," he consoled. "When I go to sleep I wish for a dream that would take me away from here. It is never fulfilled. I sleep well but I never dream. Was yours a nice dream?"

"I dreamt of a dead SS man," I said.

I knew that he could not understand the few words I had spoken, and I was much too weak to tell him the whole story. What would have been the sense of it anyway? Not one of us was going to escape from this death hut.

So I held my peace.

During the same night one of the men in our bunk died. He had once been a judge in Budapest . . . Since his death meant we would have more room in our cramped bunk we pondered whether to report his "departure"; but in the end the fact that there was a free place could not be hidden.

Two days later, when a new consignment of prisoners arrived, a young Pole was allocated to our bunk. His name was Bolek and he had come from Auschwitz, which had been evacuated in face of the Russian advance.

Bolek was a strong character and nothing could shake him. Little disturbed him, and he retained his sang-froid in the worst situations. In some ways he reminded me of Josek, although physically he hadn't the slightest resemblance to him. At first I took him to be an intelligent country lad.

At Mauthausen nobody asked a fellow prisoner where he came from or what his profession had been. We accepted whatever he chose to tell us about himself. The past was no longer important. There were no class differences, we were all equals—except for one thing: the times of our appointments with death.

Bolek told us about the men who perished on the transportation from Auschwitz to Mauthausen. They died of starvation during the endless days of railway travelling, or they collapsed from fatigue during the all-day marches. Those who could no longer walk were shot.

One morning I heard Bolek murmuring his prayers in Polish which was a very unusual occurrence. Very few of us still prayed. He who is incessantly tortured in spite of his innocence soon loses his faith . . .

Gradually I learnt that Bolek who had studied theology, had been arrested outside the seminary in Warsaw. In Auschwitz he endured the most inhuman treatment, for the SS knew that he was a priest in training and never tired of inventing new humiliations for him. But his faith was unbroken.

One night as he lay awake beside me in the bunk, I told him about my experience in the Lemberg hospital.

"After all, they are not all exactly alike," he said when I had finished. Then he sat up and stared straight in front of him in silence.

"Bolek," I insisted, "you who would have been a priest by now if the Nazis had not attacked Poland, what do you think I ought to have done? Should I have forgiven him? Had I in any case the right to forgive him? What does your religion say? What would you have done in my position?"

"Stop. Wait a minute," he protested. "You are overwhelming me with questions. Take it easy. I realise that this business sticks in your memory although we have been through so much, but I take it that your subconscious is not completely satisfied with your attitude at the time. I think I gathered that from what you said."

Was this true? Did my unrest come from my subconsciousness? Was this what drove me again and again to think about the encounter in the hospital? Why had I never been able to put it behind me? Why was the business not finished and done with? That seemed to me the most important question.

Some minutes passed in silence, although Bolek's eyes never left mine. He too seemed to have forgotten time and place.

"I don't think that the attitude of the great religions to the question of forgiveness differs to any great extent. If there is any difference then it is more in practice than in principle. One thing is certain: you can only forgive a wrong that has been done to yourself. Yet on the other hand: Whom had the SS man to turn to? None of those he had wronged were still alive."

"So he asked something from me that was impossible to grant?"

"Probably he turned to you because he regarded Jews as a single condemned community. For him you were a member of this community and thus his last chance."

What Bolek was saying reminded me of the feeling I experienced during the dying man's confession: at that time I really was his last chance of receiving absolution.

I had tried to express this view when discussing the affair with Josek but he managed to convince me otherwise at the time. Or was it illusion?

But Bolek continued: "I don't think he was lying to you. When one is face to face with death one doesn't lie. On his deathbed he apparently returned to the faith of his childhood, and he died in peace because you listened to his confession. It was a real confession for him—even without a priest . . .

"Through his confession, as you surely know—though it was not a formal confession—his conscience was liberated and he died in peace because you had listened to him. He had regained his faith. He had become once again the boy who, as you said, was in close relation with his Church."

"You seem to be all on his side," I protested. "Very few SS men were brought up as atheists, but none retained any teachings of their Church."

"That's not the question. I thought a lot about this problem when I was in Auschwitz. I argued with the Jews there. And if I survive this camp and ever get ordained priest, then I must reconsider what I have said about the Jews. You are aware that the Polish Church in particular was always very anti-semitic . . . But let us stick to your problem. So this Lemberg fellow showed signs of repentance, genuine, sincere repentance for his misdeeds—that at least is how you described it."

"Yes," I answered, "I am still convinced of that."

"Then," Bolek pronounced solemnly, "then he deserved the mercy of forgiveness."

"But who was to forgive him? I? Nobody had empowered me to do so."

"You forget one thing: this man had not enough time left to atone for his crime; he had no opportunity to expiate the sins which he had committed."

"Maybe. But had he come to the right person? I had no power to forgive him in the name of other people. What was he hoping to get from me?"

Without hesitation Bolek replied, "In our religion repentance is the most important element in seeking for-giveness . . . And he had certainly repented. You ought to have thought of something: here was a dying man and you failed to grant his last request."

"That's what is worrying me. But there are requests that one simply cannot grant. I admit that I had some pity for the fellow."

We talked for a long time, but came to no conclusion. On the contrary, Bolek began to falter in his original opinion that I ought to have forgiven the dying man, and for my part I became less and less certain as to whether I had acted rightly.

Nevertheless the talk was rewarding for both of us. He, a candidate for the Catholic priesthood, and I, a Jew, had exposed our arguments to each other, and each had a better understanding of the other's views.

When at last the hour of freedom struck, it was too late for so many of us. But the survivors made their way homeward in groups. Bolek too went home and two years later I heard that he had been ill, but I never learned what happened to him eventually.

For me there was no home to return to. Poland was a cemetery and if I were to make a new life I couldn't start it in a cemetery, where every tree, every stone, reminded me of the tragedy which I had barely survived. Nor did I want to meet those who bore the guilt for our sufferings.

So soon after the liberation I joined a commission for the investigation of Nazi crimes. Years of suffering had inflicted deep wounds on my faith that justice existed in the world. It was impossible for me simply to re-start my life from the point at which it had been so ruthlessly disrupted. I thought the work of the commission might help me regain my faith in humanity and in the things which mankind needs in life besides the material.

In the summer of 1946 I went on a journey with my wife and a few friends to the neighbourhood of Linz. We spread a rug on the hillside and looked out on the sunny landscape. I borrowed a pair of binoculars and studied nature through them. Thus at least I could reach with my eyes objects to which my weak legs could no longer carry me.

As I looked around I suddenly saw behind me, a bush and behind the bush a sunflower. I stood up and went slowly towards it. As I approached I saw other sunflowers were growing there and at once I became lost in thought. I remembered the soldiers' cemetery at Lemberg, the hospital and the dead SS man on whose grave a sunflower would now be growing . . .

When I returned, my friends looked at me anxiously. "Why are you so pale?" they asked.

I didn't want to tell them about the haunting episode of the hospital in Lemberg. It was a long time since I had thought about it, yet a sunflower had come to remind me. Remind me of what? Had I anything to reproach myself for?

As I recalled once more the details of the strange encounter I thought how lovingly he had spoken of his mother. I even remembered her name and address which appeared on the bundle containing his possessions.

A fortnight later on my way to Munich, I took the opportunity to pay a visit to Stuttgart. I wanted to see the SS man's mother. If I talked with her, perhaps it would give me a clearer picture of his personality. It was not curiosity that inspired me but a vague feeling of duty . . . And perhaps the hope of exorcising for ever one of the most unpleasant experiences of my life.

At that time the world was seeking for a more precise

understanding of the Nazi atrocities. What at first nobody could believe, chiefly because the mind could not comprehend the enormity of it, slowly became authenticated by fresh evidence. It gradually dawned that the Nazis committed crimes which were so monstrous as to be incredible.

But ere long priests, philanthropists and philosophers implored the world to forgive the Nazis. Most of these altruists had probably never even had their ears boxed, but nevertheless found compassion for the murderers of innocent millions. The priests said indeed that the criminals would have to appear before the Divine Judge and that we could therefore dispense with earthly verdicts against them, which eminently suited the Nazis' book. Since they did not believe in God they were not afraid of Divine Judgment. It was only earthly justice that they feared.

Stuttgart, I found, was one great ruin. Rubble was everywhere and people were living in the cellars of bombed houses merely to have a roof over their heads. I remembered the "Crystal Night" when they were burning the synagogues, and somebody had said: "Today they burn down the synagogues, but one day their own homes will be reduced to rubble and ashes."

On columns and walls I saw notices posted by families who had been torn apart and were seeking to find each other again. Parents were looking for their children; children their parents.

I inquired for the street in which the SS man's mother was supposed to be living. I was told that this part of the city had been devastated by the bombs and the inhabitants had been evacuated. As there was no public transport, I set out on foot to pursue my quest. Finally I stood outside an almost completely destroyed house, in which only the lower floors seemed partly inhabitable.

I climbed the decrepit, dusty stairs and knocked on the shattered wooden door. There was no immediate response and I prepared myself for the disappointment of an unfulfilled mission. Suddenly the door opened gratingly, and a small, frail old lady appeared on the threshold.

"Are you Frau Maria S——?" I asked.

"Yes," she answered.

"May I speak to you and your husband?"

"I am a widow."

She bade me come in and I looked around the room, the walls of which were cracked and the plaster on the ceiling was loose. Over the sideboard hung, not quite straight, a photograph of a good-looking, bright-eyed boy. Around one corner of the picture there was a black band. I had no doubt this was the photograph of the man who had sought my forgiveness. He was an only son. I went over to the photo and looked at the eyes that I had never seen.

"That is my son, Karl," said the woman in a broken voice. "He was killed in the war."

"I know," I murmured.

I had not yet told her why I had come, indeed I had not yet made up my mind what I wanted to say. On the way to Stuttgart many thoughts had run through my head. Originally I had wanted to talk to the mother to check the truth of the story he had told me. But was I not secretly hoping that I might hear something that contradicted it? It would certainly make things easier for me. The feeling of sympathy which I could not reject would then perhaps disappear. I reproached myself for not having planned to open the conversation. Now that I confronted the mother I did not know how to begin.

I stood in front of Karl's portrait in silence: I could not take my eyes off him. His mother noticed it. "He was my only son, a dear good boy. So many young men of his age are dead. What can one do? There is so much pain and suffering today, and I am left all alone."

Many other mothers had also been left all alone, I thought. She invited me to sit down. I looked at her grief-stricken face and said: "I am bringing you greetings from your son."

"Is this really true? Did you know him? It is almost four years since he died. I got the news from the hospital. They sent his things back to me."

She stood up and opened an old chest from which she took the very same bundle the hospital nurse had tried to give me.

"I have kept his things here, his watch, his notebook and a few other trifles . . . Tell me, when did you see him?"

I hesitated. I did not want to destroy the woman's memory of her "good" son.

"Four years ago I was working on the Eastern Railway at Lemberg," I began. "One day, while we were working there, a hospital train drew up bringing wounded from the east. We talked to some of them through the windows. One of them handed me a note with your address on it and asked me to convey to you greetings from one of his comrades, if ever I had the opportunity to do so."

I was rather pleased with this quick improvisation.

"So actually you never saw him?" she asked.

"No," I answered. "He was probably so badly wounded that he could not come to the window."

"How then was he able to write?" she questioned. "His eyes were injured, and all the letters he sent to me must have been dictated to one of the nurses."

"Perhaps he had asked one of his comrades to write down your address," I said hesitatingly.

"Yes," she reflected, "it must have been like that. My son was so devoted to me. He was not on specially good terms with his father, although he too loved our son as much as I did."

She broke off for a moment and looked around the room.

"Forgive me, please, for not offering you anything," she apologised, "I should very much like to do so, but you know how things are today. I have nothing in the house and there is very little in the shops."

I stood up and went over to her son's photograph again. I did not know how to bring the conversation round again to him.

"Take the photograph down if you like," she suggested. I took it carefully down from the wall and put it on the table.

"Is that a uniform he is wearing?" I asked.

"Yes, he was sixteen at the time and in the Hitler Youth," she replied. "My husband did not like it at all: he was a convinced Social Democrat, and he had many difficulties because he would not join the Party. Now I am glad he didn't. In all those years he never got any promotion; he was always passed over. It was only during the war that he was at last made manager, because all the younger men were called up. Only a few weeks later, almost exactly a year from the day on which we received news of our son's death, the factory was bombed. Many lost their lives—including my husband."

In a helpless, despairing gesture she folded her hands together.

"So I am left all alone. I live only for the memories of my husband and my son. I might move to my sister's, but I don't want to give up this house. My parents lived here and my son was born here. Everything reminds me of the happy times, and if I went away I feel I should be denying the past."

As my eyes came to rest on a crucifix which hung on the wall, the old lady noticed my glance.

"I found that cross in the ruins of a house. It was buried in the rubble, except that one arm was showing, pointing up accusingly to the sky. As nobody seemed to want it I took it away. I feel a little less abandoned."

Had this woman too perhaps thought God was on leave and had returned to the world only when he saw all the ruins? Before I could pursue this train of thought, she went on: "What happened to us was a punishment from God. My husband said at the time of Hitler's coming to power that it would end in disaster. Those were prophetic words: I am always thinking about them . . .

"One day our boy surprised us with the news that he had joined the Hitler Youth, although I had brought him up on strictly religious lines. You may have noticed the saints' pictures in the room. Most of them I had to take down after 1933—my son asked me to do so. His comrades used to rag him for being crazy about the Church. He told me about it reproachfully as if it were my fault. You know how in those days they set our children against God and their parents. My husband was not a very religious man. He rarely went to church because he did not like the priests, but he would allow nothing to be said against our parish priest, for Karl was his favourite. It always made my husband happy to hear the priest's praise . . ."

The old lady's eyes filled with tears. She took the photograph in her hand and gazed at it. Her tears fell on the glass . . .

I once saw in a gallery an old painting of a mother holding a picture of her missing son. Here, it had come to life.

"Ah," she sighed, "if you only knew what a fine young fellow our son was. He was always ready to help without being asked. At school he was really a model pupil—till he joined the Hitler Youth, and that completely altered him. From then on he refused to go to church."

She was silent for a while as she recalled the past. "The result was a sort of split in the family. My husband did not talk much, as was his habit, but I could feel how upset he was. For instance, if he wanted to talk about somebody who had been arrested by the Gestapo, he first looked round to be sure that his own son was not listening . . . I stood helplessly between my man and my child."

Again she sank into a reverie. "Then the war began and my son came home with the news that he had volunteered. For the SS; of course. My husband was horrified. He did not reproach Karl—but he practically stopped talking to him . . . right up to the day of his departure. Karl went to war without a single word from his father.

"During his training he sent us snapshots but my husband always pushed the photos aside. He did not want to look at his son in SS uniform. Once I told him, 'We have to live with Hitler, like millions of others. You know what the neighbours think of us. You will have difficulties at the factory.'

"He only answered: 'I simply can't pretend. They have even taken our son away from us.' He said the same thing when Karl left us. He seemed to have written Karl off as his son."

I listened intently to the woman and I nodded occasionally, to encourage her to continue. She could not tell me enough.

I had previously talked to many Germans and Austrians, and learned from them how National Socialism had affected them. Most said they had been against it, but were frightened of their neighbours. And their neighbours had likewise been frightened of them. When one added together all these fears, the result was a frightful accumulation of mistrust.

There were many people like Karl's parents, but what about the people who did not need to knuckle under, because they had readily accepted the new regime? National Socialism was for them the fulfilment of their dearest wishes. It lifted them out of their insignificance. That it should come to power at the expense of innocent victims did not worry them. They were in the winners' camp and they severed relations with the losers. They expressed the contempt of the strong for the weak, the superman's scorn for the sub-human.

I looked at the old lady who was clearly kind-hearted, a good mother and a good wife. Without doubt she must often have shown sympathy for the oppressed, but the happiness of her own family was of paramount importance to her. There were millions of such families anxious only for peace and quiet in their own little nests. These were the mounting blocks by which the criminals climbed to power and kept it.

Should I now tell the old lady the naked truth? Should I tell her what her "good" boy had done in the name of his leaders?

What link was there between me, who might have been among her son's victims, and her, a lonely woman grieving for the ruin of her family amid the ruins of her people?

I saw her grief and I knew my own grief. Was sorrow our common link? Was it possible for grief to be an affinity?

I did not know the answers to these questionings.

Suddenly the woman resumed her recollections.

"One day they fetched the Jews away. Among them was our family doctor. According to the propaganda, the Jews were to be re-settled. It was said that Hitler was giving them a whole province in which they could live undisturbed among their own people. But later I heard of the brutality with which the SS treated them. My son was in Poland at the time and people talked of the awful things that were happening there. One day my husband said: 'Karl is with the SS over there. Perhaps the positions are reversed and he is now treating our doctor, who formerly treated him—'

"My husband would not say what he meant by that. But I knew he was upset. I was very depressed."

Suddenly the old lady looked at me intently.

"You are not a German?" she ventured.

"No," I replied, "I am a Jew."

She became a little embarrassed. At that time all Germans were embarrassed when they met Jews.

She hastened to tell me:

"In this district we always lived with the Jews in a very peaceful fashion. We are not responsible for their fate."

"Yes," said I, "that is what they all say now. And I can well believe it of you, but there are others from whom I won't take it. The question of Germany's guilt may never be settled. But one thing is certain: no German can shrug off the responsibility. Even if he has no personal guilt, he must share the shame of it. As a member of a guilty nation he cannot simply walk away like a passenger leaving a tramcar, whenever he chooses. It is the duty of Germans to find out who was guilty. And the non-guilty must dissociate themselves publicly from the guilty."

I felt I had spoken sharply. The lonely widow looked at me sadly. She was not the person with whom one could debate about the sins and the guilt of the Germans.

This broken woman, so deeply immersed in grief, was no recipient for my reproaches. I was sorry for her. Perhaps I should not have raised the issue of guilt.

"I can't really believe the stories that they tell," she went on. "I can't believe what they say happened to the Jews. During the war there were so many different stories. My husband was the only person who seemed to have known the truth. Some of his workmen had been out east setting up machinery, and when they came back they told of things even my husband would not believe, although he knew that the Party was capable of anything. He did not tell me much of what he had heard. Probably he was afraid I might gossip unthinkingly, and then we get into trouble with the Gestapo, who were already ill-disposed towards us and kept a watchful eye on my husband. But as our Karl was with the SS they did not molest us. Some of our friends and acquaintances got into trouble— they had been denounced by their best friends.

"My husband told me once that a Gestapo official had been to see him at the works, where foreigners were employed. He was inquiring into a case of sabotage. He talked to my husband for a long time, and finally said, 'You are above suspicion, for your son is with the SS.'

"When Father came home and told me what had happened, he said bitterly: 'They have turned the world upside down. The one thing that has hurt me more than anything else in my life is now my protection.' He simply could not understand it."

I gazed at the lonely woman sitting sadly with her memories. I formed a picture of how she lived. I knew that from time to time she would take in her arms her son's bundle, his last present, as if it were her son himself.

"I can well believe what people said—so many dreadful things happened. But one thing is certain, Karl never did any wrong. He was always a decent young man. I miss him so much now that my husband is dead..." I thought of the many mothers who were also bereft of their sons.

But her son had not lied to me; his home was just as he had described it. Yet the solution of my problem was not a single step nearer...

I took my leave without diminishing in any way the poor woman's last surviving consolation—faith in the goodness of her son.

Perhaps it was a mistake not to have told her the truth.

Perhaps her tears might help to wash away some of the misery of the world.

That was not the only thought that occurred to me. I knew there was little I could say to this mother, and whatever I might have told her about her son's crime she would not have believed.

She would prefer to think me a slanderer than acknowledge Karl's crime.

She kept repeating the words: "He was such a good boy", as if she wished me to confirm it. But that I could not do. Would she still have the same opinion of him if she knew all?

In his boyhood Karl had certainly been a "good boy". But a graceless period of his life had turned him into a murderer.

My picture of Karl was almost complete. His physical likeness too was now established, for in his mother's home I had at last seen his face.

I knew all about his childhood and I knew all about the crime he had committed. And was pleased with myself for not having told his mother of his wicked deed. I convinced myself that I had acted rightly. In her present circumstances, to take from her her last possession would probably have also been a crime.

Today, I sometimes think of the young SS man. Every time I enter a hospital, every time I see a nurse, or a man with his head bandaged, I recall him.

Or when I see a sunflower...

And I reflect that people like him are still being born; people who can be indoctrinated with evil. Mankind is ostensibly striving to avert catastrophes; medical progress gives us hope that one day disease can be conquered, but will we ever be able to prevent the creation of mass murderers?

The work in which I am engaged brings me into contact with many known murderers. I hunt them out, I hear witnesses, I give evidence in courts—and I see how murderers behave when accused.

At the trial of Nazis in Stuttgart only one of the accused showed remorse. He actually confessed to deeds of which there were no witnesses. All the others bitterly disputed the truth. Many of them regretted only one thing that witnesses had survived to tell the truth.

I have often tried to imagine how that young SS man would have behaved if he had been put on trial twenty-five years later.

Would he have spoken in court as he did to me before he died in the Dean's room? Would he openly admit what he had confessed to me on his deathbed?

Perhaps the picture that I had formed of him in my mind was kinder than the reality. I never saw him in the camp with a whip in his hand, I saw him only on his deathbed—a man who wanted absolution for his crime.

Was he thus an exception?

I could find no answer to that question. How could I know if he would have committed further crimes had he survived?

I have a fairly detailed knowledge of the life story of many Nazi murderers. Few of them were born murderers. They had mostly been peasants, manual labourers, clerks or officials, such as one meets in normal everyday life. In their youth they had received religious instruction; and none had a previous criminal record. Yet they became murderers; expert murderers by conviction. It was as if they had taken down their SS uniforms from the wardrobe and replaced them with their consciences as well as with their civilian clothes.

I couldn't possibly know their reactions to their first crimes, but I do know that every one of them had subsequently murdered on a wholesale scale.

When I recall the insolent replies and the mocking grins of many of these accused, it is difficult for me to believe that my repentant young SS man would also have behaved in that way . . . Yet ought I to have forgiven him? Today the world demands that we forgive and forget the heinous crimes committed against us. It urges that we draw a line, and close the account as if nothing had ever happened.

We who suffered in those dreadful days, we who cannot obliterate the hell we endured, are for ever being advised to keep silent.

Well, I kept silent when a young Nazi, on his deathbed, begged me to be his confessor. And later when I met his mother I again kept silent rather than shatter her illusions about her dead son's inherent goodness. And how many bystanders kept silent as they watched Jewish men, women, and children being led to the slaughterhouses of Europe?

There are many kinds of silence. Indeed it can be more eloquent than words, and it can be interpreted in many ways.

Was my silence at the bedside of the dying Nazi right or wrong? This is a profound moral question that challenges the conscience of the reader of this episode, just as much as it once challenged my heart and my mind. There are those who can appreciate my dilemma, and so endorse my attitude, and there are others who will be ready to condemn me for refusing to ease the last moments of a repentant murderer.

The crux of the matter is, of course, the question of forgiveness. Forgetting is something that time alone takes care of, but forgiveness is an act of volition, and only the sufferer is qualified to make the decision.

You, who have just read this sad and tragic episode in my life, can mentally change places with me and ask yourself the crucial question, "What would I have done?"

Book Two

The Symposium

On the following pages appear the replies of the many eminent persons who were invited to express an opinion on the moral issue posed in the story of *The Sunflower*. The contributions by Edward H. Flannery, Milton R. Konvitz, Martin E. Marty, John M. Oesterreicher, and Cynthia Ozick were requested especially for this edition.

René Cassin

In my view the most important element consists in the fact that this confession of atrocious crimes committed against Jews by the young, dying SS man, this request for pardon with which you were faced, occurred during the war and whilst tortures and massacres were still being perpetrated.

The fear of encouraging, even indirectly, the continuation of such criminal practices completely justified the refusal of forgiveness which resulted from your fight with your conscience.

Even if, by virtue of the secret nature of the request made of you, there was no risk of your pardon leading other living criminals to glimpse the possibility of going unpunished, your refusal could not be humanly blamed. Alas, war constitutes a whole! If humanity decrees that we do not kill off a wounded soldier, it does not go as far as imposing on a man whose utterly innocent family and religious brothers are persecuted, hounded, deported to camps and finally killed, the obligation of granting forgiveness in mid-combat. The position of the man who takes part in the fight can in no way be compared with that of religious ministers, in particular with that of a minister of the faith in which the dying criminal has been brought up.

If one envisages the criminal's confession and death as taking place at a date immediately following the cessation of hostilities, the situation is different, for an individual pardon no longer takes with it the serious risk of encouraging fresh massacres. The emotional element itself is modified: the resentment felt by the man who has lost people belonging to him towards the criminal of whose number the dying man might have been remains legitimate. But it is no longer necessarily the dominant psychological factor.

The hope of a return to reason on the part of a collectivity, all of whose members were not criminals and whose young, innocent components must not be burdened with the crimes of their fathers, may be taken into account even in favour of certain criminals who were incited to evil and are now filled with sincere repentance.

But even in this case, one must grant to individuals who belong to the victim collectivities complete freedom of judgment.

On the other hand, the nation itself and social groups cannot to any extent whatsoever, under the pretext that the state of war is at an end, whitewash as a whole the instigators of crimes against individual persons. The zealous repression of crimes against humanity is a duty unlimited by time, not so much as a measure of revenge but as a means of preventing criminals from reacquiring high social positions, in the certainty that they can rear their head with impunity, and preparing means of revenging their final defeat and beginning afresh their deadly deeds of hatred and violence.

You chose in your letter to allude to a matter of conscience which I personally had to resolve, some years ago, when the

Law Faculty of Mainz University sounded me to see if I would accept, should the occasion arise, the title of "Doctor Honoris Causa" of the University by reason of my activities for the Rights of Man; all this when, during the Second World War, nineteen of my relations on my father's side in Nice and eight of my family on my mother's side in Bayonne, amongst whom were several former soldiers and invalids of the First World War, were killed in battle or deported and assassinated as Jews by the German invaders.

It is true that I myself had a grave struggle with my conscience which I finally resolved by accepting the Doctorate, followed by a journey to Mainz. But the situation with which I was faced was fortunately less crucial than that in which you found yourself. The Law Faculty at Mainz, revived under the French Occupation in 1948 after more than a century's inactivity, could not have incurred any responsibility during the war: it could not be accused of having constituted a centre of chauvinistic education and incitement to war. Quite the contrary; one of the chief aims pursued by its founders and actively pursued since, was to create a link on the banks of the Rhine between the German and French cultures and to work at the reconciliation of the two peoples.

I was brought consequently to wonder if it was not my duty to overcome my personal grudges as a French Jew in order to contribute to the effort together with such well-intentioned German teachers. I had already adopted the position amongst those who approved of the government of the State of Israel of accepting and even requesting material reparation from official Germany.

Having considered that it was my duty to share for my part in a task which would have bearing on the future, I accomplished it to the full. Far from forgetting the barbaric conditions in which so many cherished members of my family had perished, I made a point of recalling these conditions in the speech I delivered in Mainz, in order to stress to what extent the French were anxious to live in a state of lasting peace with a German people who, for its part, would actively shun all solidarity with its criminal constituents.

As you can see, the decision I took in 1962–3, almost twenty years after the cessation of the massacres, delicate as it was, and one which I would repeat if it had to be remade, entailed motives for which one could find no parallel in your case.

This is why the opinion I expressed above is completely devoid of any direct relationship with the personal matter I have just recalled.

David Daiches

The problem posed in this story is complicated by the fact that the author is at pains to establish the background of the young Nazi's home life and development and this involves the reader in something more than a simple judgment of a given situation. One of the most difficult problems facing modern man is to decide on the degree to which full psychological and sociological understanding of a criminal could or should make us less prone to judge his actions. The French proverb "tout comprendre c'est tout pardonner" sums up this aspect of the problem but it does not really clarify it.

One does not need to be a behaviourist psychologist in order to see that every human action can be "explained" in some degree in psychological or sociological terms or in both. The implications of this dilemma are very complex, but all I wish to say here is that both the individual and society must retain the power of judging human actions however much we respect the attempt to explain them, because without moral judgment there simply can be no pattern of civilised behaviour underlying a culture and there can be no incentive on the part of individuals to refrain from giving way to sadistic and similar impulses if they can simply attribute them cheerfully to psychological or sociological or even physiological factors.

It has been said that you can turn a murderer into a saint by removing part of the frontal lobe of his brain, and even if this is literally true it cannot alter the fact that murderers are bad and saints are good. So the first point I want to make is simply that the story becomes involved in the larger issue of the relation between explanation and understanding on the one hand and refusal to judge on the other, and this is a very complex problem indeed.

In a sense, as so many of our psychiatrists now tell us, all criminals are sick, but to infer from this that we ought to treat them as Samuel Butler suggests in his novel *Erehwon* is not to make a helpful contribution to society.

The other question raised by the story is whether one has a right to forgive on behalf of others somebody who has wilfully inflicted the most appalling miseries on human beings. The question here, it seems to me, revolves around the meaning of the word "forgiveness". There are two sides in this matter of forgiveness. The forgiver can purge himself of feelings of anger and hatred and revenge by a conscious decision to consider the matter closed, while the forgiven can feel at peace with himself when the person whom he has injured forgives him. But in most cases these are verbal formulas.

There is some sense in the idea adopted by most of the higher religions that only God can forgive, because a true moral offence is an offence against divine order in the universe. As between human beings, it seems to me that forgiveness is a formula for eliminating unprofitable brooding on the one hand and self-reproach on the other, and as such I suppose it is socially necessary. I know in the little things of life everyone feels better when they throw away a grudge and decide to start all over again. It is not so easy with the kind of crimes committed in Nazi concentration camps.

In so far as someone who has committed such a crime or series of crimes asks an individual other than a representative of God to forgive him the request is a device for obtaining psychological comfort, and it may be that we have an obligation to give such psychological comfort to a dying man. I think that in the position of the hero of this story I would have given that comfort, as to do so would harm nobody and help the guilty individual.

But I don't think that this is forgiveness. I think in such a circumstance a man might say to the dying criminal who has committed such atrocious crimes against that man's people that he understands now how individuals not intrinsically wicked or beastly could under certain circumstances be drawn into committing wicked and beastly acts. He should offer understanding, which is a kind of forgiveness. But I don't see how in any genuinely meaningful sense one individual can offer forgiveness for crimes that were not committed against him.

There is not much point in saying to a murderer "I forgive you for murderering my friend's children" or to a robber "I forgive you for robbing the bank next door". So I think I would solve the problem by drawing a distinction between understanding and forgiveness, at least in a case like this.

But I confess that I am not certain if this really is a helpful attitude to take up, and the moral problem remains very troubling.

Constantine FitzGibbon

You ask me, because of the political, philosophical and religious import of your own experience: "Was I right or wrong?" You are thereby asking me to sit in judgment upon your actions, or to be more precise upon your failure to act, in circumstances of horror, long ago. You are, by extension, asking me to judge the dying SS man, and, by further extension, his mother. I shall do my best to answer your question, but I must refuse the role of judge. I do so neither on principle nor for fear of the responsibility that every act of judgment entails, but merely because of a lack of competence.

In writing *The Sunflower* you are honestly telling the truth about yourself, so far as you can understand that truth, and you are honest enough to know that you cannot understand all that truth. I must try to return that compliment, before I try to answer your question.

I am neither a Jew nor a German. You say that in your childhood and youth, even before the Nazi vileness, you never met anyone who was not conscious of your own Jewishness. I am one of the people you never met in those days. In the Western upper-middle-class world in which I grew up, my family and the circles in which I moved were of course aware of Jews, but not aware that there was any "Jewish problem", and when I first went to Germany, as a boy of 15 in 1935, and first heard anti-semitic talk, it struck me, quite simply, as utterly ridiculous. Of course I had heard Jewish "jokes" but they were no more anti-semitic than were similar Italian "jokes" or French ones or the much rougher mockery that we heard about the Germans. Therefore I had no reason to be an inverted racist, a philo-semite. Of course as a young man interested in philosophy and history I had some, though no great, interest in the Jewish religion and in the history of the Jews: greater than in that, say, of the Chinese: less than in that of the Greeks: comparable, perhaps, to the much smaller history of my own people, the Irish. (I am not a Roman Catholic, and until quite recently regarded religious thought as an interesting subject for intellectual investigation: I do so no longer.) Therefore, in my private life, until I married a Jewish wife at the age of 40 it never occurred to me to *search* for any difference between Jew and Gentile, either in my friends or in the arts. That my son is in part Jewish gives me, when I bother to think about it, pleasure because it is likely to be an enrichment.

But if I am not a racist in any way—or so at least I flatter myself, and I am here talking about African and Asian racism too—I am increasingly not an anti-racist, save in so far as I would once again volunteer, as I did in 1939, on September 3rd of that year, to fight against sadistic murderers who used so absurd a creed as Nazism in order to realise their wicked fantasies. My emotions towards those people then were stronger but of the same quality as those that I have felt since towards Stalinists and Mao-ists. People who put lies into action become, inevitably, murderers, since they must make the facts fit the "truth" as they imagine it to be: and they have no knowledge of truth and eventually, like your SS man, are forced to admit that it has all been lies. That is why he was forced, at last, to pray *through* you.

Why do you repeat his prayer, to me? I know neither you nor him. I can only guess from my reading, from my friends, from an increasing interest in what makes us turn to God.

Had I been in your position, a condition which I find almost inconceivable—but not quite—I think I would have done what you did in that room in the Technical High School. I would then have been twenty-three years old, and I would have felt, I think, that he was offering too easy a chance for revenge through pity. (This is, of course, omitting the personal conditions of extreme terror and partial resignation to that terror.)

Today, I think, though now the circumstances are quite inconceivable to me, I would have reacted with Christian brutality, for today, to me, Eli and the boy in Taganrog and my son Francis would be one, and I would remember Christ's remark that it would be better that a millstone be put about his neck and he were cast into the sea than that he should harm one of these little ones: and I think I would strangle him in his bed.

I shall finish soon. I have said that I am no sort of racist. This does not mean that we are not basically affected in our thoughts and deeds by the Faiths in which we, or our parents, or even our ancestors were brought up. Your anxiety about your own actions is the anxiety of your religion. I have the greatest respect for you that you have spoken it to the world, all the more so since I can imagine what agony it must be so to do. The greatest European crime of our time must not be allowed to rest quietly beneath a sunflower.

A critical moral question is posed in *The Sunflower:* should Simon, a Jewish internee in the concentration camp, have expressed to Karl, a repentant and dying SS man, the forgiveness Karl had requested of him?

The problem is sharply formulated by the author in these words of Arthur, a friend of Simon and a fellow internee:

> 'And you ... do stop talking about it. All this moaning and groaning leads to nothing. If we survive this camp—and I don't think we will—and if the world comes to its senses again, inhabited by people who look on each other as human beings, then there will be plenty of time to discuss the question of forgiveness. There will be votes for and against, there will be people who will never forgive you for not forgiving him. . . . But anyhow nobody who has not had our experience will be able to understand fully. When we here argue about this problem, we are indulging in a luxury which we in our position simply cannot afford.'

> Arthur was right, I could see that. That night I slept soundly ... (pp. 77–78).

Simon's sleep was not to remain so tranquil. Before the story draws to a close, we find him still wrestling with the problem.

In a sense the author of *The Sunflower* indicates his answer to the problem in Simon's subsequent behavior. The extent to which Simon was driven to search out Karl's mother after the war is eloquent testimony of the depth of the guilt he was experiencing. The actual meeting with Karl's mother brings other clues to light. He refuses to reveal to her Karl's true character and deeds, tempted as he was to reveal them. One senses in Simon through this reluctance a definite spirit of atonement, though he does not acknowledge or recognize it as such.

In the final analysis, what are we to think of Simon's refusal to grant Karl the forgiveness he begs of Simon?

I find it impossible to defend, and I must be satisfied with understanding it without approving it. I should like nevertheless to focus on the moral issue rather than on the emotional or psychological factor: Can one morally and with full deliberation refuse forgiveness to a repentant sinner?

It is a cardinal principle of the Judaeo-Christian ethic that those who sincerely repent should be granted forgiveness. One need not belabor the Hebrew and Christian scriptures for exhortations to and examples of forgiveness. They are endless.

There is not a single instance in the Hebrew scriptures in which reference is made to an "unforgivable sin." Nor does the New Testament contain any such reference except in the controverted allusion to the "unforgivable sin against the Holy Spirit" (Mark 3:28). It is clear that forgiveness of repented sin is one of the basic concepts underlying the Judaeo-Christian morality as well as universal natural ethics. This moral imperative of universal scope might be called a moral archetype of the human psyche. It was neither a Jew nor a Christian but an Oriental sage who wrote, "If hate is met with hate, where will it all end?" To refuse pardon after repentance is a form of hate, however disguised.

The author of *The Sunflower* connives with this principle, though obliquely, when, speaking of those bystanders who watched Nazi atrocities, he writes, "was it not just as wicked for people to look on quietly and without protest at human beings enduring such shocking humiliation? But in their eyes were we human beings at all?" Does not Simon watching the dying Nazi in his final agony pleading for mercy also fit this description of inhumanity? Atrocities need not always be physical. Or does Simon also think that the dying man is not human?

The book brings up the question of whether Simon had a right to forgive Karl in the name of all Jews. This consideration seems to be an attempt to extenuate Simon's refusal to forgive. It appears to me irrelevant. The dying SS man did not ask that Simon speak in the name of all Jews. The notion of extending forgiveness to include a general and wide-ranging forgiveness on the part of all Jews was a construction of Simon and his friends. The real situation called for forgiveness by one Jew, any Jew. The situation was personal and intimate; the question of the collective right to speak for all Jews was a public and juridical one that does not apply to the actual circumstance. I cannot see how this supposedly collective right to forgive can be used as a justification for the refusal by Simon and his advisors and it is another indication of their unrecognized feelings of guilt.

One could argue moreover that if Karl inflated in his mind the forgiveness conceded by Simon as an individual to the proportions of a collective forgiveness, this would be his own doing, not Simon's. Should Karl die under the happy illusion of collective forgiveness, one is permitted to ask "Where would be the harm?"

The most important ethical question in *The Sunflower* is whether the demands of morality are exceptionable in the context of total moral evil, complete dehumanization. Should human conscience and integrity not transcend a condition of complete demoralization? Or again, is not the failure to transcend this condition another triumph for the brutalizing and dehumanizing process?

Finally, while conscious of the vast differences in the respective situations and culpabilities involved, we may ask whether Simon and his advisors did not themselves participate in Karl's sin.

Herbert Gold

I have read *The Sunflower* with the shock that recollection of these events will never fail to awaken in me.

I believe the SS man had no right to ask your forgiveness. To deal with you as a symbol for all Jews was a part of his disease. I believe you followed a proper and human path in your reaction to his confession. No one has the right to judge you for your refusal to comfort this particular dying man who chose you to do him the service of easing his spirit. Your silence and withdrawal seem absolutely just. It is not cruel unless leaving a man to examine his own soul is cruel.

Should your heart have led you to another response to him, one of generosity to him—or later of harshness to his mother in telling her the truth—I believe these too would be justifiable responses. The guilt for this horror lies so heavily on the Germans of that time that no personal reaction to it is unjustifiable. I'm not speaking of planned acts of revenge, of course, nor of a guilt which involves more than those who acquiesced in the crimes. But the human responses of those who suffered directly can be judged, if they need to be judged, only in individual cases.

No one has the right to command forgiveness for these crimes, but probably—so complicated is the human fate—no one has the right to forbid it, either. For myself, I fear something abstract and unfeeling in any general decision about a horror which consists of millions of individual moments and murders.

Mark Goulden

The Sunflower is remarkable for many reasons. In its own right it is a moving, sorrowful, terrifying narrative which holds the reader enthralled as it unfolds.

It tells of a tragic experience in the life of the author, Simon Wiesenthal, whose memorable book (*The Murderers Among Us*) dealt with the German war criminals who tried to escape retribution. But apart from its own narrative value *The Sunflower* is remarkable because it poses a searing question that will challenge the moral conscience of the reader.

The question is concerned with forgiveness—specifically, forgiveness towards the Germans for crimes which they committed, less than thirty years ago. Some may say that the whole subject is slightly jejune nowadays, for there is evidence that the world has conspired to forget the monstrous atrocities that shamed mankind and made a mockery of religion and humanity, even though they occurred well within living memory.

I always find it difficult to exercise restraint when I write or think about these fearful crimes. The mind begins to boggle at the sheer enormity of it all. Is it true, one asks oneself, that civilised human beings actually built huge, complex death-chambers for the express purpose of destroying millions of other human beings like vermin?

Can it really be that ordinary German soldiers obeyed orders to machine-gun long rows of living people standing at the edge of vast open graves into which the riddled bodies fell in grotesque heaps?

Did the Germans actually feed into their gas chambers over 960,000 innocent children—a number that is equivalent (if you want a visual cognate), to ten Wembley Stadiums filled to capacity with kids under thirteen?

Do our eyes deceive us when we watch those films of the shuffling, living skeletons wandering around mountains of shrivelled corpses in the camps of Belsen, Auschwitz, Birkenau, Treblinka, etc., etc.? Were these zombies once ordinary normal human beings like you and me?

To reflect on these things is to plunge oneself into a nightmare of unbearable ghastliness. The human mind is incapable of comprehending the magnitude and the mathematics of such slaughter. But, alas, it isn't a nightmare. It's all too dreadfully true and it is all recorded, in minute detail, in the vast literature on the subject that now exists.

Just ponder this item for instance: At the recent Auschwitz trial in Frankfurt a dispute arose as to the exact number of victims who were massacred in that death camp. Finally it came out in evidence that of 4,400,000 men, women and children (approximately the entire population of Denmark) who were condemned to Auschwitz, only 60,000 were still alive when the camp was liberated. Which means that 98.5 % of all the deportees were methodically exterminated by the Germans. This arithmetic of butchery, this harvest of death, would stagger the imagination even if the carnage concerned rats, never mind human beings.

Well, that was the burden of guilt which the Germans bore when the war ended, and for this culpability they have made no act of atonement as a nation. One often asked in the early days, whether a people who had done these things—either by active participation or silent acquiescence—could ever live down such a legacy of inhumanity. Dare they ever lift up their heads again in civilised Society? Would the brand of Cain stay for ever on the German brow just as the tattooed Star of David would remain indelible on the arms of many a victim who escaped?

These were questions which only time could answer, and time indeed has answered them. For it is a fact that within a matter of three decades, that nation which perpetuated the greatest massacre of human souls in all history—virtually before the very eyes of the world—that nation has been able to resume its place in the comity of peoples with utter self-assurance and complete composure, actually being welcomed by the President of America as "our devoted, staunch and honourable ally".

Today, people don't talk any more about the mass murder of six million human beings. They don't even want to read about it any longer. Books on the subject are now categorised disparagingly as "concentration-camp stuff" and as such are virtually unsaleable. The world seems to have agreed to "let the matter drop" and nobody has more sedulously promoted this "forget it" campaign than the Germans themselves—not for any piacular reasons, but simply "to restore our good name", as Adenauer once naïvely put it. They even tried recently to introduce a law to stop any more Nazi trials because these served only to perpetuate the legends of the gas-chambers, the crematoria and the torturings.

By a sort of tacit consent the very nomenclature of Germany's misdeeds has, over the years, been modified so that euphemisms such as "the Holocaust", "The Final Solution", "Genocide", etc., are now used to mask the inherent and stunning horror of what is plainly massacre, slaughter and bestiality. And we are reminded always that it was the Nazis—a mythical horde of sub-humans from outer space—who did it all. They descended, unbidden, on the most highly sophisticated, Kultured nation on earth and issued orders which they dare not, could not, and *did not* disobey. Apparently no living German was ever a Nazi; very few even saw one, and whatever atrocities did happen, took place during what is known as the "Hitler Era"—or in the "time of the Nazis"—which is the greatest collective alibi ever conceived.

Small wonder then, that the world should so quickly forget crimes (which nobody ever saw) committed by external criminals (whom nobody ever knew)?

To forget all, may be easy, but to forgive all, must be something more than a pulpit platitude. First, we must ask ourselves in whose hands lies the privilege of granting forgiveness? We can, of course, say, with the ecclesiastics, that mercy and forgiveness belong entirely to God, in which case the whole dialogue comes abruptly to an end. Or we can subscribe to the dictum of the poet Dryden— "Forgiveness, to the injured doth belong". But, unfortunately, the injured in this case (six million martyred dead) are incapable of exercising such prerogative or indeed of expressing any opinion at all.

And if the dead can't forgive, neither can the living. How can you possibly forgive monsters who burned people alive in public; in ceremonies, staged in the open, with typical Teutonic pomp and precision? Could we even expect the Almighty to exonerate them? But it is precisely a hideous crime like this, that is central to the challenging question posed in *The Sunflower*—was Wiesenthal right in refusing to forgive the dying Nazi? You can ignore the question, or evade it, or hedge it about with casuistic hair-splitting, but the simple issue remains—what would you have done in Wiesenthal's shoes? There is no generic answer; it is an individual dilemma that demands a personal answer.

I, for one, would have had no hesitation in solving the problem. I figure it this way: Wiesenthal himself was about to die—ignominiously and forgotten—as a direct result of all those "ideals" and those "standards" which the dying Nazi and millions like him were proud to defend and fight for. I would have asked myself what might the young Nazi have become had he survived or, indeed, if Germany had won the war? I would have tried to visualise the Christ-like compassion and pity which the victorious Germans would have bestowed on the new million Wiesenthals now in their power. And reflecting on these things, I would have silently left the deathbed having made quite certain there was now one Nazi less in the world!

Hans Habe

On reading *The Sunflower* I was greatly excited, as everybody who reads your story must be. However, you have not asked me for literary criticism, but for my views on the problems of forgiveness. The two unspoken questions in your story interest me specially: whom ought we to forgive, when ought we to forgive? I imagine that you did forgive the man whom you call Karl S. But that is, I fear, too simple an answer. We are not an appeal court from God. He revises our judgments, we do not revise His. God's punishment struck the SS man, bypassing all human courts. He whom men punish can still be acquitted by God: he whom men acquit God still may punish. But he whom God has punished we cannot acquit nor can we increase the Divine punishment. Least of all through hatred. He who has been punished is removed from our jurisdiction, even the words "Requiescat in pace" are a mere suggestion. We can hope that a person may rest in peace, we cannot ensure it.

Immediately there arises the question: ought we, can we, forgive others, murderers who are still alive?

Here too we must be more precise. Whom do you understand by "we"? If you mean the Jews, mothers and fathers, relatives and friends of the martyred and slaughtered people, then there is a considerable shift of meaning. Murder is neither forgivable nor unforgivable. Morals are not restricted to the victims. I have always doubted the role of so-called counsel who appear on behalf of private individuals in murder cases. To judge crimes against humanity is the affair of humanity. Victor Gollancz, the English publisher, who immediately after the war wrote the word "Forgiveness" on the Jewish flag, was for me just as dubious as are the Jews who take the sword of revenge from the hand of humanity. By "we" I mean humanity, not the Jews alone.

Is murder unforgivable? Yes, without question. Can one forgive the murderer? That is a question that is closely tied up in the complex of punishment. A desire to punish the murderer is the commandment of Justice. To forgive the murderer after he has suffered punishment is the commandment of Love. You write that Karl was "not born a murderer and did not want to die a murderer". What has that to do with the problem of forgiveness? It is not relevant and in no sense an excuse. Practically nobody is born a murderer. Those who are born murderers are the pathological exceptions—their deeds, as a matter of fact, are more pardonable than those who are born "healthy". The death of Christ on the Cross is the symbol of a free human decision. He who decides to commit a murder is laden with a greater guilt than he who is driven to become a criminal by abnormal environment. Anyhow, there is hardly anybody who wanted to die a murderer, even atheists are afraid of the Hereafter.

So we cannot forgive murderers—so long as the murder is not atoned for, either by us as jurymen or by the Supreme Judge. Every society—every society, I repeat, rests upon certain moral principles, at the head of which stands atonement for capital crimes, and this brings me to your next unspoken question: can there be any extenuating circumstances for murder?

It stands to reason there must be extenuating circumstances—otherwise every murder trial would be pointless—so we must examine them. In several passages, particularly in your conversation with the SS man's mother, you describe Karl's path to murder. That is the natural, but complicated, thing to do. One must not confuse the question of forgiveness with the question of punishment. If Karl were being tried by an earthly court, there would be such extenuating circumstances in his favour as youth, environment, the times, the general atmosphere, and war conditions. Nevertheless, in this case we are operating in two different dimensions. Forgiveness is a spiritual matter, punishment is a legal matter. The verdict of the court is influenced by extenuating circumstances. Such circumstances induce a milder judgment, but in no way mean that we are forgiving the murderer. The free will given to a man does not merely grant him the choice between committing a murderous deed or refraining from it. It is also a part of man's free will whether he allows justice to take its course or whether he dispenses with it. An amnesty granted to an unpunished murderer is a form of complicity in the crime. It does not foster forgiveness, it precludes it.

Again, who should be the object of our forgiveness or our revenge?

You are a man of high principle, and although you relate the story of the SS man and his victims, the proceedings which initially were directed against the murderer, end with the Nazi system as the prisoner at the bar. Here our paths diverge.

For the regime we are discussing there is no "problem" of forgiveness. The crimes of the regime were unforgivable, the regime has been tried and destroyed. Meanwhile we are faced not with Mephistopheles, but with Faust. Corruption, though a force of permanent duration, cannot exist without collaboration from the corrupted. The corrupted, in a word, are not victims of the corrupters, but collaborators. With the words "Terrible vision!" Faust turns away, but the ghost rightly defends himself: "You invited me cordially, you have long dabbled in my domain ... You have passionately striven to see me, to hear my voice, to gaze on my countenance ..."

The firm is Faust & Co. or, if you prefer it, Mephistopheles & Co., partners just like Hitler and Karl S. The proof lies in the counter-proof. The devilish Nazist regime did not corrupt everybody, and of those whom it corrupted most stopped at murder. I cannot accept the excuse that the system relieves the individual of responsibility. Walt Whitman says: "To the States, or to any individual State, or to any city among the States, offer strong resistance and little obedience!" Resistance to evil is not heroism but a duty. Anyone who thinks that he can get rid of evil "in itself" in the world is a victim of megalomania, and who knows whether megalomania in itself does not contain the germs of evil? The important thing is to strengthen the resistance to evil.

Here, in my view, lies the true problem of forgiveness, and here perhaps we approach the answer as to whom we ought to forgive and when.

Mankind will stay as it is—in itself a terrible prospect—if the principles of love and justice remain obstinately separated instead of complementing each other. Looking on the question from this angle, you will find that in the history of man since the beginning of Creation, love and justice have opposed each other. At one period justice was the human ideal, at another, love. The divine idea of justice in love, love in justice, mankind has magnanimously left to the Creator.

Forgiveness is the imitation of God. Punishment too is an imitation of God. God punishes and forgives, in that order. But God never hates. That is the moral value worth striving for, but perhaps unattainable.

You write, at the end of *The Sunflower*, "I know that many will understand me and approve of my attitude to the dying SS man. But I know also that just as many will condemn me because I refused to ease the last hours of a repentant murderer."

I belong to neither class of reader. It seems to me immaterial whether you forgave the SS murderer or not, for Providence relieved him of life and punishment, and your conscience from the burden of decision. But at least you did not hate the dying murderer, and that is a beginning. To forgive without justice is a self-satisfying weakness. Justice without love is a simulation of strength.

One of the worst crimes of the Nazist regime was that it made it so hard for us to forgive. It led us into the labyrinth of our souls. We must find a way out of the labyrinth—not for the murderers' sake, but for our own. Neither love alone expressed in forgiveness, nor justice alone, exacting punishment, will lead us out of the maze. A demand for both atonement and forgiveness is not self-contradictory; when a man has wilfully extinguished the life of another, atonement is the prerequisite for forgiveness. Exercised with love and justice, atonement and forgiveness serve the same end: life without hatred. That is our goal: I see no other.

Friedrich Heer

The human disasters of the recent past and of the present day, which disgrace mankind again and again, like a chain reaction after the genocide and racial murders of the Hitler era, draw one's attention to a great failure.

At the time, and often enough nowadays, there is a lack of consciousness and conscience. A restricted and undeveloped consciousness and a restricted and undeveloped conscience frequently overlook the words "Cain, where is Abel thy brother?"

The slaughter, the killings in the street, the harassing and humiliations of the "others" are now simply not realised. Neither yesterday nor today is there any realisation. Very probably (certainly, in my opinion) there is an intimate connection between the stifling of conscience in the post-war period and the present-day complicity in genocide. Such complicity may consist merely of oily phrases of "condolence" and turning away in stupid silence. Yesterday's genocide gives birth to today's. Conscience aroused by yesterday's genocide would have produced altered conditions and a different climate of opinion—a human climate, in which the murderous jungles of genocide would have been unable to exist. Up to the present time no such climatic alteration has been created—we live in a hothouse atmosphere of murder and suicide—consequently every effort to impress our consciousness with the murders and genocide of the past, and compel it to analyse them, is of inestimable value.

The model genocide of our era, Murder No. 1, is the slaughter of the Jews under Hitler. Simon Wiesenthal, in his story *The Sunflower*, carrying many autobiographical details, poses the following question for debate. Can, or should, an individual, a Jew, forgive a wholesale murderer of his fellow-Jews—murder which did not concern him personally, e.g., the murder of his own child, his wife, his mother, his brothers and sisters.

The untruthfulness and deep corruption of our times are shown not least in a lying and entirely false call for reconciliation. A pseudo-humanism and a superficial, verbose Christianity cries at the top of its voice: "Put an end to the trials! Away with the complicated and incomprehensible past! Yes, leave them in peace after all this time, the poor devils, they have atoned enough." They mean yesterday's murderers who, unharmed, have long since returned to the bosom of their families and their comfortable jobs. Such false, lying appeasers, with their oily phrases, want to besmirch man's true dignity. The true dignity of man consists of persistence to the end in the effort to solve the great human problems and again and again to tread the Way of the Cross. Each and every one carries the responsibility. Where are you going? What will you do next? You must make up your minds—without regard for security, responsible only to the voice of your conscience.

From this problem, from this "crucial" situation, the great majority of people fled yesterday and flee today. Few have any idea even of the existence of the problem, the "crucial" situation which Wiesenthal has exposed in his *Sunflower*.

Adolf Hitler seduced millions with his assurance that he would take personal responsibility for everything that happened in the war. The truth is that a man, whatever his position in life, is only one individual, carrying a personal and peculiar responsibility on which his task in life and his human dignity are based. He can give only a short answer to our problem: he can and must be responsible for his own life, and he bears a certain measure of responsibility for the life and death of his nearest and dearest. The individual cannot assume responsibility for the crimes committed by others.

The Roman Catholic Church offers confession, the sacrament of penance, and absolution. For the murderer who repents and has confessed, the priest can grant absolution and the remission of punishment for his sin. God alone, however, can grant final remission for mortal sin. The priest acts only as God's "deputy".

The debate over this "deputy" question has not yet tackled this problem: How far can the murderers of the Hitler era actively and effectively receive absolution? In my view it is more than probable that the priestly confessors have all too lightly granted absolution to many a prominent SS murderer, and to other war criminals.

This problem, however, is outside the question raised by Simon Wiesenthal, though it throws some light on it. When the Jews were *in extremis*, when indeed the human situation was at its worst, God was "on leave". Or at least a long way away, if indeed he was anywhere to be found. That is indeed,

127

the feeling that the great majority of people still have today. "God" does not relieve mankind or the individual of responsibility. It is now clear that a man, in the case of serious crime, has no authority to forgive mortal sins which another has committed against other people. He, the individual, can provide a certain presence, a certain "being on the spot", like the witness to the SS man's confession. From his mere, silent presence it is possible that healing powers—metaphysically healing powers—flowed into the dying murderer. For me personally such effect is most probable, though beyond all human calculation. The ethics of *The Sunflower* are in no way affected by speculation about such possible "solutions", and that seems to me a particularly valuable asset of the book.

The sun of Simon Wiesenthal's *Sunflower* has the fiery breath of the desert sun. It singes everything that is "humane" and "all-too-humane". Thus in the desert, in the night of humanity, stand the three persons, facing each other but divided by gulfs and abysses—the young murderer, the man of the people of Israel, and the third is the invisible God, who cannot be reached or talked over by pious phrases. This God has assigned to man a responsibility which he, the man, in this last desperate case cannot carry. Paradox of Godhead, paradox of humanity! Both are incapable of elucidation. For both there is no "solution", no "redemption", and without it one must resign oneself to remaining unenlightened, watchful, and in pain.

Gustav W. Heinemann

Last week I gave up my post as Federal Minister of Justice and now have a few weeks of private life in front of me before taking over my new office. I thus have time at last to read *The Sunflower* and write to you about it.

First of all I must say that I was greatly moved by your encounter with the dying SS youth and later with his mother. How remarkable are the dispensations of Providence, which, I cannot put it otherwise, rule the lives of us all!

In my judgment there was a link between the two encounters. You took your leave of the mother "without taking from the poor woman the last thing that remained to her: the belief that she had had a good son". You kept from her what you knew about her son—two things, first that he was a murderer who did not want to be a murderer, but that "a merciless ideology" had made a murderer out of him, and secondly that he was looking for forgiveness through repentance and confession to you. The truth about the son must include both elements. The two elements, taken together, would have utterly destroyed the mother's false picture of an ideal son and at the same time would have given her a true picture of him as (in spite of everything) forgiven.

You did not succeed in conveying both truths to the mother. That too disturbs you, just as it disturbs you that you were unable to respond to the confession of the dying murderer by a word of forgiveness or pardon or relief from his burden. So I must agree with what Bolek, the Pole, said to you.

The conflict between Justice (in the form of Law) and Forgiveness is the thread that runs through your story. Justice and

Law, however essential they are, cannot exist without Forgiveness. That is the quality that Jesus Christ added to Justice and with which He gave it life. Such are my feelings in the matter.

Abraham J. Heschel

Over fifty years ago, the rabbi of Brisk, a scholar of extraordinary renown, revered also for his gentleness of character, entered a train in Warsaw to return to his home town. The rabbi, a man of slight stature, and of no distinction of appearance, found a seat in a compartment. There he was surrounded by travelling salesmen, who, as soon as the train began to move, started to play cards. As the game progressed, the excitement increased. The rabbi remained aloof and absorbed in meditation. Such aloofness was annoying to the rest of the people and one of them suggested to the rabbi to join in the game. The rabbi answered that he never played cards. As time passed, the rabbi's aloofness became even more annoying and one of those present said to him: "Either you join us, or leave the compartment." Shortly thereafter, he took the rabbi by his collar and pushed him out of the compartment. For several hours the rabbi had to stand on his feet until he reached his destination, the city of Brisk.

Brisk was also the destination of the salesmen. The rabbi left the train where he was immediately surrounded by admirers welcoming him and shaking his hands. "Who is this man?" asked the salesman. "You don't know him?" "The famous rabbi of Brisk." The salesman's heart sank. He had not realised who he had offended. He quickly went over to the rabbi to ask forgiveness. The rabbi declined to forgive him. In his hotel room, the salesman could find no peace. He went to the rabbi's house and was admitted to the rabbi's study. "Rabbi," he said, "I am not a rich man. I have, however, savings of three hundred rubles. I will give them to you for charity if you will forgive me." The rabbi's answer was brief: "NO".

The salesman's anxiety was unbearable. He went to the synagogue to seek solace. When he shared his anxiety with some people in the synagogue, they were deeply surprised. How could their rabbi, so gentle a person, be so unforgiving. Their advice was for him to speak to the rabbi's eldest son and to tell him of the surprising attitude taken by his father.

When the rabbi's son heard the story, he could not understand his father's obstinacy. Seeing the anxiety of the man, he promised to discuss the matter with his father.

It is not proper, according to Jewish Law, for a son to criticise his father directly. So the son entered his father's study and began a general discussion of Jewish law and turned to the laws of forgiveness. When the principle was mentioned that a person who asks for forgiveness three times, should be granted forgiveness, the son mentioned the name of the man who was in great anxiety. Thereupon the rabbi of Brisk answered:

I cannot forgive him. He did not know who I was. He offended a common man. Let the salesman go to him and ask for forgiveness.

No one can forgive crimes committed by other people. It is therefore preposterous to assume that anybody alive can extend forgiveness for the suffering of any one of the six million people who perished.

According to Jewish tradition, even God Himself can only forgive sins committed against Himself, not against man.

The Sunflower, whether wholly autobiographical or in parts fictional, is an intensely moving and vivid book. Were it my task to write a literary criticism of it, I should be loud in its praise. But the request that has been made of me is to give an opinion on one definite point. Did the author do right in refusing a word of compassion to the dying SS man who had made to him the confession of the atrocious murder of a Jewish child?

The author does not admit of any repentance for his refusal. But his two Jewish friends, now dead, thought that he would have done very wrong to have admitted such compassion. Only the Polish seminarist thought otherwise and he has vanished from the author's life so that he is no longer able to keep in touch with the developments of his thought. But it is clear from the author's visit to the SS man's mother that his mind is not at ease. It is indeed not clear what purpose that visit had or what purpose he could have supposed that it would have had, since he was not willing to tell the mother the truth about her son, but the fact that he made it is proof of a disturbed, uncertain and restless mind.

I am asked what, absolutely, he ought to have done under these circumstances. Let me first make it clear that that is quite a different question from the question "what would I have done?" To that second question I can make no answer. I claim no capacity to resist temptation above the average and what fortitude I would have been able to show in face of horrors so incomparably greater than any that I have ever been called on to face I cannot say. We can all say that men ought to be martyrs if challenged on their faith. We can none of us say whether in the day of trial we ourselves would have the hardihood to be martyrs.

But on the absolute challenge what the author should have done I have no doubt that he should have said a word of compassion. The theology of the matter is surely clear and, as the Polish seminarist truly says in this book, there is no difference on it between Christians and Jews. Differences are here irrelevant. The law of God is the law of love. We are created in order to love one another, and, when the law of love is broken, God's nature is frustrated. Such bonds when broken should be reforged as soon as possible. We are under obligation to forgive our neighbour even though he has offended against us seventy times seven.

On the other hand we are all born in original sin. (Jewish orthodoxy, I understand, does not admit that exact phrase but the language in which they repudiate it shows very effectively that they do in fact believe in it as much as any Christians.) Indeed one could not well do otherwise, for original sin, unlike the other Christian doctrines, is a definite necessity of thought. Men are born in sin and when God has been defied by actual sin there cannot be forgiveness unless there is repentance. We are indeed told to be reluctant to condemn others. "Judge not that ye be not judged". It is our duty to reflect how small is our own understanding and that, if we knew all of a story, we should often see how much more there was to be said for another's action, how much more—it may be—of the blame really is ours than appeared at first sight.

But these considerations, so often just, are here irrelevant. Here the SS man had committed an appalling crime. It was perhaps relevant for him to recount the impulses that had caused him to join the SS, the appalling corruption of Nazi propaganda to which he had been subjected, the military discipline of which he was the slave at the time of the act, but these are explanations. They are not excuses. The SS man does not pretend that they are excuses. He does not attempt to excuse himself. He was guilty of an appalling crime and he was frankly confessing his crime. Nor has the author any doubt of the sincerity of his repentance. Therefore, however difficult it was, there is surely no doubt that a word of compassion, indicative of his recognition of that sincerity, should have been said.

It is of course true that penitence involves a willingness to make restitution to the person wronged and, had the circumstances been other, it would have been reasonable to have demanded of the SS man that, even if he could not bring back to life the little child whom he had killed or discover any of his immediate relatives, yet he should in some notable way have attempted some service to the Jews which would have given evidence of the sincerity of his repentance. Whether he could or would have satisfied such a challenge had he lived and been restored to health, who shall say? Since he was to die in a few hours, the question is meaningless. Even if the author had doubted, one should give the benefit of the doubt.

'Tis God shall repay. I am safer so.

Nor indeed is it easy to see, as indeed the author himself confesses, for what reason the SS man should have sent for and made this confession to a Jew unless he was sincerely ashamed of what he had done.

Of course I am stating what seems to me to be the absolute moral law. I am not suggesting that obedience to that law could under the circumstances possibly have been easy or passing any personal condemnation. But surely the absolute moral law was stated by Christ at the Crucifixion when He prayed for the forgiveness of His own murderers. It is of course true that the persecution and murder of Jews was still going on and that the author fully expected that he himself would be murdered before long. But that, I should have thought, in the moral order made forgiveness easier rather than more difficult.

The author's two Jewish friends, Arthur and Josek argued with him that maybe he had a right to forgive injuries against himself but that he had no right to forgive injuries against other people. But in so far as this act was not merely a personal act of one SS man against one Jewish child but an incident in a general campaign of genocide, the author was as much a victim—or likely to be soon a victim—of that campaign as was the child, and, being a sufferer, had therefore the right to forgive. His forgiveness could not in the nature of things be the casual, idle word of someone who pardoned without caring the perpetrator of a distant crime to which he was really indifferent.

Nor of course has forgiveness anything to do with the refusal to punish. In this case since the SS man was just about to die the question of punishment did not arise, but, had he survived, the fact that he had been spiritually forgiven would of course have been no reason why he should not have been subjected to the appropriate punishment.

It is interesting to understand why the SS man wanted thus to confess to an unknown Jew. The SS man had been brought up as a Catholic but he had abandoned his religion when he joined the Hitler Youth. There seems some suspicion that on his deathbed he had a certain return of faith—or at least a desire to return to his faith. If that was at all so, if he had come to think that there was at least a possibility of future life and a judgment awaiting him, then it would of course have been reasonable that he should have confessed to a priest had one been available. If there were no priest he could be confident that the verdicts of God would be just and, if his repentance was sincere, need be under no fear that God would not show mercy.

Whichever way round, why was his state made any better, his mind at all relieved, by confessing to an unknown Jew? The Jew had no power to give him absolution. It is not easy to see but it is a psychological fact that sinners on their death-bed do often wish to relieve themselves by telling their story to someone and under any normal circumstances who would be so hard-hearted as to refuse to listen to such a story?

The real issue is whether the Jew and Nazi were two of God's children sharing a common humanity or whether they are two different sorts of being, irrevocably at war with one another. If the second interpretation was that accepted by the Jews it was assuredly the Nazis who were responsible for it and they could not complain if the Jews accepted it. Yet for all that, whatever the temptation to think otherwise, it is surely the inevitable consequence of any monotheistic faith that all men—even the least naturally loveable—are the children of God, in Christian belief that they are those for whom their Omnipotent Creator did not disdain to die, in Jewish belief that they are God's creatures.

One can well understand how the Jews in their camps had come to tell one another in the bitter sick joke which the author recounts to us that God was on leave. Yet it was pre-cisely the rejection of this blasphemy that surely religious faith demanded—demanded the belief that somehow, however diffi-cult it might be to see how, "God is not mocked" and that, as with Job, "though He slay me yet will I trust in him".

Man, what is this and why art thou despairing?

God shall forgive thee all but thy despair.

According to an old mediaeval legend the Apostles assem-bled together in heaven to recelebrate the Last Supper. There was one place vacant, until through the door Judas came in and Christ rose and kissed him and said "we have waited for thee".

We might as well make one thing clear before we start: not only is there no possible answer to Simon Wiesenthal's awful question, there is quite simply no answer which we would be justified in giving. By the very fact that there exists, at community level, such a thing as justice, any occurrence not covered by this judicial system is left exclusively to the judgment of the individual affected by this occurrence.

Let us imagine that I have been the victim of a road-hog. The community will settle the question on the material plane, demanding such and such a compensation, imposing such and such a punishment. But I shall remain the sole arbiter and judge of my feelings towards the road-hog. Nobody will have the right to demand that I forgive him: nobody would have the right to reproach me in any way whatsoever should I refuse to forgive; and my revenge itself, should I decide to avenge myself, would concern society only in so far as my action had infringed its laws but not in so far as it had been the expression of a feeling on my part. All this which is true of minor offences is even truer of actual crimes, and all the more so of that crime of crimes: the systematic slaughter of innocent people.

Since nobody therefore has the right to tell Simon Wiesenthal that he was wrong in refusing to forgive his SS man, nobody is any more justified in telling him he was right. This is obvious. And the fact that Simon Wiesenthal himself seeks the opinion of his friends makes no difference to the root of the problem: anyone who declared him to be justified would be assuming thereby the right to criticise him also. Well, nobody has this right nor can Wiesenthal grant it to anyone, for this would be to bestow upon a human being the unacceptable right to inspect another person's conscience.

It being impossible to tackle the problem as it was put, I tried looking at it from a different angle. I asked myself not whether I approved or disapproved of Wiesenthal, but what I would have done in his place. This new question implied that it would be possible for me to put myself in his place; in other words into the skin of a deportee.

The only thing is, I was never deported. I was an officer, and five years a prisoner of war in an Oflag. Can I make the extension from one situation to the other? Our prison resembled that of the deportees in that, like them, we were almost cut off from the world and, if I may say so, maintained on the same food rations. But we differed from them in that every month we were entitled to four letters or cards and two food parcels of about a stone. Our supply of mail and parcels having ceased upon our disembarkation, we came to know the same hunger and the same moral isolation as they. On this plane then I could understand without too much effort the feelings of a deportee.

But I have overlooked the most important point. Never in the course of those five years did I suffer any injury to my person. When a German officer (and I was dealing with people from the Wehrmacht, not SS men) spoke to me, they called me "Sir". When I was summoned to the Abwehr on a charge of carrying false papers and attempted escape, I was not strung up on a butcher's hook. In short, I was not treated as an underdog, and death itself, threatening as it was during those five years, bore no relationship to the death that struck out at random amongst the deportees. In short, I know just enough about all this to assure myself most categorically that *I have no right* to put myself in the place of a deportee: imagination has its limits. The only people who can speak as deportees are those who were deported.

Having made these reservations, I can now move on a little; for in no way did I wish to avoid the question I was asked. Quite the contrary; I wish to answer it with all my wits about me and with complete lucidity. But this will involve a great many "ifs". Up to my release in April 1945, I had had no idea of the horrors of concentration camps: I simply suspected that they were no joyride. Had I encountered Wiesenthal's SS man at that time, I would doubtlessly have forgiven him: out of ignorance. I was set free on the moors at Luneberg; we were re-housed by the English in Bergen and it was here that we came to hear of what had been going on in Belsen, the camp nearby. Had I met the SS man then, I think I would have acted like Wiesenthal. But I would probably have regretted it afterwards. Or perhaps, on the contrary, I would, in spite of everything, have yielded to pity; but I would certainly have regretted this too afterwards . . .

After all, pity in itself has no moral value. It betrays weakness, not to say sentimentality, more often than it does fraternity. A surgeon who was struck with pity would not dare to touch the wound . . . What I mean to say is that, even knowing what I knew after the Bergen-Belsen episode, it is possible that, being more sensitive to the atrocious suffering of this dying young man than to my extremely hazy awareness of the horrors of the deportation, I would, like a coward, have given in to pity. I say like a coward because I would have done this despite myself, despite the dictates of reason and reflection. My ensuing remorse at this cowardice of mine would have dogged me for the rest of my days.

And what if I were to meet the dying SS man today, now that the dead are cold in their graves? I would then weigh up the pros and cons; I would ask myself detachedly how the SS man's repentance and death pangs weighed in this scale of the balance, whilst in the other scale . . . No, it is impossible. Even taking the question from the angle I adopted earlier, I cannot answer Simon Wiesenthal with my reason. What would I have done in his place? I close my eyes and stop thinking, I answer blindly, I answer with my bowels: twenty years ago I would have acted as he did out of rightful revenge: today I would regret it as he does. And that too is senseless.

Thus, nonplussed, I, like Wiesenthal, questioned those around me. This only served to demonstrate further the hopelessness of any answer. How did the young feel? No forgiveness. The very old? Forgiveness. People between the two? Precisely what I said earlier: on the spur of the moment they refused to forgive; on further reflection, they thought they should have forgiven. There was, however, one exception in this last category: a man who had actually been tortured by an SS man who, between sessions, talked literature to him. This is the gist of what he said to me: "The millions of innocent people who were tortured and slaughtered would have to come back to life before I could forgive." And who can blame him? It is easy to act the do-gooder: "I forgive them and I've got the great role." But this is to condemn the dead a second time.

The young, the old, those who suffered in body (and in soul), those who did not suffer: the standpoint people take in this matter is dictated merely by their instinctive reactions. How then can we discuss the issue? Any discussion turns into hair-splitting. For example: to what extent was the young SS man sincere? To what extent would what was only a first crime with extenuating circumstances have directed the course of his life to come, either by hardening him or by awakening his conscience? To what extent did the fear of divine punishment have a part in his repentance? Had he remained deaf to the call of faith, his repentance might have been purer—but how much purer? And so on . . .

There is one last point: the most important one to my mind. When Eichmann stood for trial I suggested that there should have been as many trials as there had been murders. One trial per murder: that is, some six million trials . . . Do not shrug your shoulders: the real crime of our day lies in doing exactly this. Every one of the six million victims has a right to his own individual trial; because every victim is an individual human being and thus individually murdered. To accept a collective trial is in a sense to play the game of the slaughterers which consisted in wiping out individual people under the cover of that lifeless entity: number—the "Million Man Unit", as Jules Romains would say.

It is this very problem which is outlined in the accounts of Simon Wiesenthal and his repentant SS man. If Wiesenthal as an individual could not forgive the SS man as an individual, it is because their relationship did not and could not remain on the individual plane. The SS man represented the entire SS, the entire Nazi system, the whole of Germany, and even beyond Germany, the whole of man's evil forces. Wiesenthal for his part was not just Wiesenthal but the entire deportation, and beyond this, the bulk of the Nazi victims. Man to man, I think Wiesenthal would have forgiven in the face of so obviously sincere a repentance; one which was sanctioned, as it were, by the criminal's sufferings. He could not do so because of what he represented and what the person he was dealing with represented. As for the latter, despite his desperate attempts to be no more than an individual, he was unable to tear himself away from the SS group he embodied; this was all the less possible in that he himself was not addressing the individual standing before him, but the body of victims which this stranger represented for him. So neither of these two men were free to be himself and to assume before the other man responsibility for his own actions and no more; they symbolised quite simply, the one like the other, the one with the other, the stultifying oppression of the individual by society at a level where even the word forgiveness loses all its meaning.

The most tragic side of this drama is that by not forgiving, one opens up the way for one's own lack of humanity. Simon Wiesenthal could doubtlessly have acted in no other way than he did; but in so doing, he was denying his suppliant his individual existence. He was then morally speaking, committing the very crime committed by Nazism, or come to that, of any form of racialism. His only excuse in the last instance is that of revenge.

I am one of those people who think that there are crimes so atrocious that justice becomes ineffectual in dealing with them, turning thereby into injustice. At this point revenge—revenge in its raw state, absolutely spontaneous revenge—could well be a moral necessity. It is all very well for me to condemn the death penalty in principle, it is all very well for me to acknowledge that a sadist is merely ill; if someone with an illness of this kind were to violate my little boy for instance, I would willingly kill him and this in full awareness of the absurdity of my action. I know full well that the highest form of justice is that which reinstates the criminal instead of punishing him.

But must we not think of the victim as well even if revenge does not serve to bring him back to life and only adds one more crime to the others?

Jacob Kaplan

I want firstly to say with what pleasure I read the typescript of your work, *The Sunflower*.

One cannot begin to read it without wanting to continue to the end, as much on account of the work's literary quality as for the serious problem of conscience it poses.

I will not digress upon your personal memories which so movingly evoke your "concentrationary" life in order to come to the question upon which you chose to consult my opinion.

It would seem to be impossible not to share in the various moods through which you passed on hearing the horrible confession of the dying SS man.

As this confession unfolds itself, all the pity one might have felt for him disappears, giving way to aversion when he reveals his active participation in a massacre of Jews.

How, in effect, can one take to heart his very real moral and physical suffering when, at that very moment, tens of thousands of Jews continue to be exterminated daily by other SS men in the same way as he himself exterminated them or to be systematically murdered by Nazis in death camps?

How could one comply with his request for forgiveness when all over the place innocent victims, calling upon divine justice are endlessly and repeatedly crying out in the words of Job's exclamation: "Earth, do not cover my blood; let nothing stand in the way of my cries!"?

And yet, like you, we remain uneasy. This SS man was not one of those who experienced a sadistic joy in torturing the Jews. He bore them no hatred. He even felt compassion for what they were suffering and this commiseration he proved to them in his way by having food brought to them whenever he could. Neither was he one of those Nazis, so plentiful after the war, who had the impudence to plead not guilty, covering themselves with the pretext of having simply obeyed orders. For his part he in no way sought to diminish his responsibility. He fully recognised it. His remorse gave him no respite. And it was his feeling of guilt which was to invade his conscience when, leaving the trench and launching himself into the attack he went to meet death. As if hallucinated, he was to see running towards him the Jewish family at which he fired on the day of the massacre, the final vision preceding his mortal would.

We are therefore in the presence of an SS man who differs from the others, an SS man who bitterly regrets his crimes, and who accepts as a just punishment the cruel suffering inflicted by his wounds. He could have called upon a chaplain of his cult who would most probably have granted him absolution. But he valued the forgiveness of a Jew more highly than the absolution of a priest. It is from a Jew that he awaited the word which would have allowed him to die in peace.

What then should one have done? In my view the only people entitled to make the decision are those who were deported, those who suffered personally in mind and body the odious treatment devised by Nazi barbarism. It is precisely the opinion of one of your companions at the time for whom: "Nobody who hasn't gone through bodily what we are going through will ever be able to fully understand."

Nevertheless, in your desire to know whether you were right or wrong in not having granted the final request of the dying SS man, you expect an answer from me.

I in turn question myself and wonder on what moral basis you could have granted him forgiveness.

Of course there is the biblical commandment: "If your enemy is hungry, give him food; if he is thirsty, give him drink."

The entreaty of which you were the object was perhaps not unrelated to this religious precept which was also referring to hunger and thirst of a spiritual kind. And had it been a case of

144

your having to forgive an action, even a criminal action, committed against yourself, you would have been following the truly Jewish tradition in not refusing your pardon. You could dispose freely of this pardon which depended solely on you. But this did not apply in the case of the Nazi soldier. His crimes had been committed against others. The granting of pardon did not come within your competence, but within that of the various victims. The fact that the latter were no longer alive in no way modified this condition. You know—I do not have to tell you—that the Jewish Law teaches that sins committed against God can be absolved by sincere repentance, but for sins committed against other men we must first obtain the forgiveness of those whom we have wronged in order to be in a position to invoke divine mercy.

I think then that you would have done well to point out that it was not in your power to satisfy him, but that the sincerity of his repentance and his acceptance of death as a just punishment for his crime would certainly be taken into account in God's judgment.

In the absence of forgiveness, these words would partly have complied with what he expected of you and would at the same time have been in conformity with the Jewish tradition. At the time of the Talmud, when condemned criminals were going to be executed, they were exhorted to repent, urged to call upon divine mercy, saying: "May my death serve as my expiation."

I have the feeling that you are disturbed not so much at not having given the SS man the forgiveness you were unable to grant him as at not having given full expression to the pity you could have shown him. You naturally felt this pity towards him at several junctures. Is this not a characteristic of the Jewish soul, so much so that the descendants of the Patriarch Abraham are called: merciful, sons of the merciful?

But your pity was not expressed in words and because of this it has remained unsatisfied.

But you have no need to reproach yourself for this. The problem with which you were faced was particularly difficult to resolve; all the more so in that you had to make an urgent decision as to the course to adopt and thus in unforeseen and unusual circumstances. What would have been the attitude, 25 years ago, of those who today make known their opinions to you, after mature reflection? They cannot know themselves. Let us then be humble in our assessments, let us not permit ourselves to pass judgment; let us remind ourselves of Hillel's phrase: "Do not judge your neighbour before finding yourself in the same situation as he."

Robert M. W. Kempner

In three great processes of recent years, in which as subsidiary counsel I represented surviving relatives of the victims, I heard the statement made by the accused in the German criminal courts: "I beg you to express my deepest regret to the survivors, and through you I ask for their forgiveness."

It happened for instance in the Munich proceedings against the SS-Gruppenführer Wilhelm Harster and the SS-Sturmbannführer Wilhelm Zöpf, both of whom were accused of assisting in the murder of ten thousand Jews in Holland. Among their victims was Anne Frank with her sister Margo, and their mother, besides Edith Stein, the Carmelite nun and philosopher, and many "non-Aryan" monks and nuns. Harster said he wanted to ask the forgiveness of the relatives, including those who were not represented in court. He hoped they would accept his regrets. Zöpf, who was Eichmann's representative in Holland for Jewish affairs, associated himself with Harster's words. Both were sentenced to long terms of penal servitude (15 and 9 years respectively).

A few months later the same thing happened in Bamberg. Franz Rademacher, of Ribbentrop's Foreign Office and also engaged in Jewish affairs, was accused of assisting in the "final solution", i.e., the annihilation of thousands of Jews. He expressed to the Bamberg court his regret at what had happened. He received five years' penal servitude.

There was a third case in the Paderborn court in February 1969. The SS-Standartenführer Fredrich Grüttemeyer was accused of complicity in the murder of Felix Fechenbach, the Social Democratic Jewish editor. The murder took place on 7th August 1933 in the forest of Paderborn, many years before the beginning of the "final solution". Soon after the proceedings began I asked the accused whether he had any statement to make concerning Fechenbach's widow. He asked me to convey his deep regrets, with a request for forgiveness. At the end of the proceedings he and his counsel repeated the request. The accused was sentenced to four years as accessory to murder.

Had Hitler been victorious, would the four accused have accepted decorations and promotions as reward for their action? Now, in 1967, 1968, and 1969, they were all being tried for murder, facing not the gates of death but the prison gates. Their mental state was certainly not so abject as that of the SS man who lay dying in Simon Wiesenthal's presence. Nevertheless there were parallels between the situations.

What was the attitude of the judges? In summing up

before passing sentence they mentioned the requests for forgiveness. The President declared that the Court felt the requests were sincere and showed that the accused were no longer obstinate Nazi criminals, but that they had to some extent modified their former ideas. Therefore the declarations of the accused could and must be taken into account as extenuating circumstances. In none of these cases was a loss of civil rights imposed. Thereby the judges, in the legal sphere, pronounced a partial pardon. They had the right to do so, although it is not expressly mentioned in the penal code that a plea for forgiveness could be considered as an extenuating circumstance. In the code there are only certain provisions in cases of sincere repentance of persons convicted of treason and arson, provided that a prevention of the consequences of the deed is still possible.

What is my own attitude to the request for forgiveness? As I considered it sincere, I saw no ground for rejecting it out of hand. As agent for the victim's relatives I was legally empowered to convey the request to them, but I did not see that I was in any position to give, or justified in giving, a positive answer to the plea. I did not feel that I was competent to grant forgiveness.

The right to pardon thousands of criminal murderers is reserved for the Lord of Life and Death. Therefore, in my three court cases in Munich, Bamberg, and Paderborn, which were held in the presence of members of the public, including many schoolchildren, I pointed to the Crosses on the walls of the Court: "Whatever the earthly punishment may be, for their deeds the accused will still have to answer to the Lord in Heaven." We on this earth cannot free the evildoers from their guilt by "forgiveness". We can only pray that the Lord may have mercy on their souls. There is nothing more in our power.

Simon Wiesenthal was right when he refused to assume the powers of a Supreme Being.

Hermann Kesten

It is annoying how much one forgets, how quickly, how easily. Memory is the foundation of civilisation. Without memory we should be senseless idiots. Anyone, who after the Second World War demands that we should forgive and forget everything is expecting us to be as barbaric as the murderers, who have forgiven themselves everything and forgotten all their inhuman deeds. One must try to control one's feelings—but forget nothing nor willingly encourage one's innate forgetfulness.

Ought one to forgive? We teach our children to ask our forgiveness, even when such asking is against their own ideas and inclinations, and we forgive them. But often children do not forgive grown-ups for burdening them with the humiliation involved in an admission of bad behaviour.

We ask God to forgive our sins. Certain Jewish and Christian ideas about God have long seemed barbaric to me. How can I ask forgiveness from a God who has said that he will punish my sins to the third and fourth generation, or even from a God who has promised us heaven and invented hell and purgatory—a sadistic machinery of atonement which goes on functioning until the Last Day, if God is not prepared to forgive some sinners at least?

The Jews have a Day of Atonement, Yom Kippur, when they ask God's pardon for all the sins they have committed during the past year and to ask forgiveness from their friends, relatives, acquaintances, and enemies for any acts they may have done against them out of hatred or love or envy or jealousy or a hundred other motives.

To ask forgiveness is a very human thing to do. To have a conscience and to have feelings of remorse is a proof that one is not unfeeling, not inhuman, not (a term unjust to animals) "brutal".

To be candid, forgiveness is an act of sensual pleasure. He who forgives is filled with a delightful emotion about himself as well as about the person he is forgiving. What a charming picture it makes: the child in its mother's lap, forgiven; or the child who has forgiven its mother's faults; or the lovers who have forgiven each other all manner of things and then climb into bed together filled with pleasurable thoughts.

Nevertheless, to be willing to forgive everything, on every occasion, means that one is lacking in discrimination, in true feeling, in reasonableness, in memory.

Tout comprendre c'est tout pardonner is wrong; it should be *Tout comprendre c'est tout confondre*. To understand everything does not mean to forgive everything, it means to confuse everything, to get everything hopelessly muddled.

There must be a limit to everything, even to forgiveness. I am a firm opponent of capital punishment. I would never have executed a Hitler or an Eichmann, because I hold every killing to be inhuman, especially killings and executions carried out in the name of the law and the people.

Anyhow, whom is one to forgive? I can forgive no murderer, no executioner, no judge or jury who have passed a death sentence. Thank heaven I am not a judge. For the guilty there are laws and proper processes of law which will protect the innocent and, after consideration of all the circumstances will not punish the guilty man but will prevent him from repeating his offence against his fellow-men and the dictates of morality. In principle I do not hold with punishment.

Of course we must not reward murderers; certainly not, as sometimes happens, make them ministers in the government, or judges, or highly respected members of society.

Has any individual the right to forgive a mass-murderer? Who is entitled to speak on behalf of the victims? Is a mother acting rightly when she sees a man slaughtering her seven children before her eyes, and then forgives him because he repents—after he learns that he is dying of blood-poisoning which he acquired in the course of the slaughter?

Is there any Jew or Christian or Mohammedan or atheist who has the right to forgive the slaughter of a million Jewish children? I can forgive an adulterer if I believe that condemnation of adultery is mere prejudice. I can forgive a thousand-and-one other things, but can I forgive a deed that causes a human being to come to an untimely end?

There might be circumstances in which I too might be a murderer. Perhaps I too would have found reason to forgive myself. But I would have been wrong.

When the State forgives, and proclaims an amnesty, it is not usually considerations of justice that inspire such a step, but purely practical reasons. A State that forgives mass-murderers is on the way out.

An individual, a private person, may of course forgive somebody, if able and willing to do so. He has only to satisfy his own conscience. A man wilfully pokes another man's eye out—for a joke. The victim forgives. Then he cuts the victim's tongue out, severs a limb, smashes every bone in his body, and asks his victim whether he forgives him, even in the act of cut-ting off his head. For the butcher feels he will repent some day, and the victim nods agreement even in the act of losing his head.

It is quite extraordinary the things men will forgive each other. You cannot have a slice of bread and butter from me, but you are welcome to my life! There are patriotic mothers who can forgive their country for the heroic deaths of their sons. Many people will not forgive the man who steals a watch, but are willing to forgive entire world wars. They forgive Stalin the dead millions, they forgive Johnson the war in Vietnam, they forgive murderers, especially if they themselves run no risk of becoming victims. In fact, everybody forgives everybody anything far too often—and far too rarely.

We all live in contradiction to ourselves, in contradiction to others, in contradiction to the laws and the dictates of humanity. "Blessed are the meek: for they shall inherit the earth. Blessed are the merciful: for they shall obtain mercy. Love your enemies, bless them that curse you, do good to them that hate you, and pray for them which despitefully use you and persecute you. For if you love them which love you, what reward have ye? Do not even the publicans do the same? Be ye therefore perfect."

Thus far the Sermon on the Mount. But Christ nowhere says that one should forgive mass-murderers. True, he says: "Forgive us our debts, as we forgive our debtors." And "If ye forgive not men their trespasses, neither will your Father forgive your trespasses."

In the same sermon Christ says: "Not every one that saith unto me, Lord, Lord, shall enter into the kingdom of heaven; but he that doeth the will of my Father which is in heaven." And every tree that bringeth not forth good fruit is hewn down, and cast into the fire."

Job says: "Have I rejoiced at the destruction of him that

hated me, or lifted up myself when evil found him?" Jesus says: "Love your enemies." But does he say that one must forgive the murderers of one's children? And if he had said so, I for one would have disagreed with him.

The problem of forgiveness is unending, when one considers social conditions and the relations of a man to himself and to other people. It is possible, however, to lay down general rules, and to find solutions in individual cases from time to time.

Forgiveness is also a political problem, not only a religious, social, psychological, or intellectual question.

For example, it seems to me that in the German "Third Reich" the "writing-desk" murderers were much more dangerous and abominable than the actual torturers and executioners, and that even more dangerous and abominable were the politicians like Hitler, Goebbels, and Göring, and their accomplices like Globke, and those writers who lauded and propagated the inhuman measures, like Ernst Jünger and Gottfried Benn, Martin Heidegger, Carl Schmitt and Oswald Spengler, Hans Carossa and Hjalmar Schacht, and Alfred Rosenberg.

To forgive these intellectual traitors to humanity would be more difficult than to forgive, for instance, a twenty-year-old SS murderer of children.

In everyday life there are probably only a few people who act consistently and logically in this matter of forgiveness; who act according to their convictions.

Although as individuals we may be guided by a strict moral system and obey the moral laws, yet we are apt to form private and unconscious or unacknowledged judgments about people we encounter in public or private life.

The world, like world history, is full of good and great men who at some time or other, e.g., in their youth, have committed misdeeds but have been converted and have repented their sins. True, they have not always made reparation. There is no reparation possible for murder. Nevertheless they may have gone on to render unique services to mankind and to the cause of humanity.

I do not forgive murder, but I am grateful to history that these men survived their crimes and eventually did much more good than evil.

If I must judge Moses, for example, what I hold against him is the massacre of the Egyptians and the laws in which he approved the death sentence for women taken in adultery. I cannot forgive him for that. But I admire the man who gave us the ten Commandments, for these (though I cannot approve them in their entirety) have brought to mankind magnificent lessons and precepts, and I love the man who raised humanity several steps up the ladder of civilisation.

Milton R. Konvitz

Repentance occupies a very high place in Jewish thought. Among the seven things that were created before the creation of the world, Torah stood first, and next to it was repentance. The logic of the collocation is spelled out by George Foot Moore:

> That God did not make the Law, with all its command-
> ments and prohibitions and its severe penalties, without
> knowing that no man could keep it, nor without creating a

way by which his faults might be condoned, is as firm a conviction as there is in all the Jewish thought of God. Repentance must therefore be coeval with Law (*Judaism in the First Centuries of the Christian Era,* vol. 1, p. 266).

. . .

God knew that the man he purposed to create, with his freedom and his native evil impulse, would sin against the revealed will of God in his law and incur not only its temporal penalties in this life, but the pains of hell. He must therefore have provided beforehand the remedy for sin, repentance (ibid., pp. 526–27).

That repentance is not available to Jews exclusively is made clear by the book of Jonah, at the conclusion of which God accepts the penitence of the people of Nineveh and revokes His stern judgment against them and their city.

The Bible relates that Manasseh, when he was king in Jerusalem, committed the worst abominations, including the burning of his sons as a sacrifice to the Baals. He "seduced Judah and the inhabitants of Jerusalem, so that they did more evil than the nations whom the Lord destroyed before the people of Israel" (2 Chronicles 33). Yet when he became a penitent, God forgave him; from this incident the rabbis concluded that:

If a man were to come and say that God does not receive the penitent, Manasseh could come and testify against him, for there was never a man more wicked than he, and yet, in the hour of repentance, God received him, as it is said, "He prayed unto God, and God was entreated of him" (Numbers Rabbah, Naso, XIV).

It may be argued that all this is true of God, who is "gracious and compassionate, patient, abounding in kindness and faithfulness, assuring love for a thousand generations, forgiving iniquity, transgression and sin" (Exodus 34:6), but that this standard is too high for man to attain. On the other hand, man is commanded to live a life in the imitation of God. "Be holy, for I am holy" (Leviticus, 11:44).

Had Karl committed an injury to the person of the narrator, his deathbed, profoundly felt remorse and penitence and his plea for forgiveness would have necessitated an affirmative response from the victim. Indeed, there are some sayings of the Sages that teach even a greater measure of compassion: the victim must be beforehand with his forgiveness. Thus it is related that Mar Zutra, when he went to bed, was in the habit of saying: "Forgiven be everybody who may have done me an injury." According to the Babylonian Talmud:

> If a man has received an injury, then, even if the wrongdoer has not asked for his forgiveness, the receiver of the injury must nevertheless ask [God] to show the wrongdoer compassion, even as Abraham prayed to God for Abimelech and Job prayed for his friends. R. Gamaliel said: Let this be a sign to you, that whenever you are compassionate, the Compassionate One will have compassion upon you (Baba Kamma IX, 29, 30).

But in *The Sunflower* the problem is more complicated, for Karl's crimes were not committed against the man he was addressing from his deathbed. The narrator felt that he had not been authorized to act for the victims or for the Jewish people, nor, he felt, was he God's deputy with power to forgive.

He neither condemned Karl nor forgave him; he simply was mute in his presence.

It might be argued that his failure to forgive Karl his

crimes against others was in fact a condemnation. But this would be going too far. When a governor or president, who has the power to pardon, refuses to use it in favor of a condemned prisoner, he could then be said to affirm the judgment of guilt and the sentence. But in *The Sunflower* the narrator had no such power. His refusal to say anything in response to Karl's plea for forgiveness has, therefore, the character of a purely neutral act (or non-act).

The moral demands made of society are radically different from those that may be made of an individual. As a private person I may have the duty to overlook grievances and to forgive offenses against me, especially when the wrongdoer has confessed his wrong and has pleaded for forgiveness, and, if restitution is possible, has sought to make whole the harm he has done. But it is otherwise with a judge. A court is bound to follow the law, and to let the law run its course. Suppose Eichmann, when the charges were read to him in the court in Jerusalem, had tried to show that he was sincerely remorseful. The court would still have been bound to enter a judgment of guilt and to pass sentence upon him. Many criminals have gone to their death remorseful and penitent. The function of a court is only to determine guilt or innocence as of the time when the alleged crime was committed. The defendant's later state of mind or heart is totally irrelevant. After the defendant has been found guilty, however, the judge, in fixing the sentence, may take into consideration facts and circumstances which, at the trial, would have been sharply excluded. The judge needs to consider the gravity of the crime, but to a degree he may mold the punishment to the measure of the defendant's character, for he needs to think of the degree to which the defendant is likely to be influenced by the nature of the punishment imposed. But the court also needs to take account of the extent to which the punishment may serve as a deterrent to other persons, and the effect of the sentence on public opinion. But no matter how much weight he may give to the criminal's subsequent feelings of sorrow and contrition, the judge has no power of pardon; the sentence must stop short of that and must fall between the maximum and minimum penalties fixed by law. The power of pardon is usually vested only in the head of state.

Whatever weight one may wish to give to the concept of utility in any theory of punishment, there are cases where the retributive theory must be said to have a dominant place, and in such cases Kant's famous statement is altogether relevant and convincing:

> Even if a civil society were to dissolve itself by common agreement of all its members (for example, if the people inhabiting an island decided to separate and disperse themselves around the world), the last murderer remaining in prison must be executed, so that everyone will duly receive what his actions are worth and so that the bloodguilt thereof will not be fixed on the people because they failed to insist on carrying out the punishment; for if they fail to do so, they may be regarded as accomplices in this public violation of legal justice (*The Metaphysical Elements of Justice,* trans. John Ladd, sec. 333).

Kant would not recognize in such a case the right of a sovereign to grant a pardon, for, according to Kant, the right of pardon can be exercised only when the crime committed has been against the sovereign himself; he cannot exempt from punishment anyone who has committed a crime against a subject, for in the latter case "exemption from punishment constitutes the greatest injustice toward his subject" (Ibid., sec. 337). Generally, mankind has not, however, followed Kant in imposing such rigid limits on the power of pardon. But there is, I believe, well-nigh universal recognition of the principle that the power of pardon is an executive and not a judicial function.

Well, now, our analysis has, I believe, shown the following propositions:

1. The narrator in *The Sunflower* has no power or right to pardon Karl for crimes against others or against the Jewish people.

2. The narrator is not God's deputy and, therefore, cannot presume to act as if he were God. He has no power to bind on earth what shall be bound in heaven, or to loose on earth what shall be loosed in heaven (Matthew 16:19).

3. He is not a judge who can find Karl innocent because of his repentance and remorse—no judge has that power.

4. He is not a sovereign and has no power of pardon vested in him by the community to which Karl's victims belonged.

Having said all this, we have not, however, said all. Guilt and innocence are not terms confined within legal and judicial limits. Hitler was never brought to justice, but who would hold back from saying that Hitler was guilty of the most heinous crimes? The historical and the private judgment has also its rights and duties. The extra-judicial record may be just as full and conclusive as that made at a trial in court.

And by the same token, there is an extra-constitutional right and duty of pardon, vested in the historical and private judgment.

From this point of view, what we have in *The Sunflower* is a man writhing in physical and spiritual agony, on the verge of death, filled with painful remorse. He is suffering what Kant called natural punishment (*poena naturalis*): "In natural punishment," wrote Kant, "vice punishes itself . . ." (op. cit., sec. 331). Karl saw the narrator as a Jew, that is, that he was in some sense representative of the victims, from whom Karl pleaded for understanding and forgiveness. What should have been the response?

It seems to me, though I say this with diffidence and hesitation, that in this encounter the spirit of the Jewish tradition called upon the narrator to say to Karl: "I cannot speak for your victims. I cannot speak for the Jewish people. I cannot speak for God. But I am a man. I am a Jew. I am commanded, in my personal relations, to act with compassion. I have been taught that if I expect the Compassionate One to have compassion on me, I must act with compassion toward others. I can share with you, in this hour of your deep suffering, what I myself have been taught by my teachers: 'Better is one hour of repentance in this world than the whole life of the world to come' (Avot, IV, 17). 'Great is repentance, for it renders asunder the decree imposed upon a man' (Babylonian Talmud, Rosh Hashana, 17b). It is not in my power to render to you the help that could come only from your victims, or from the whole of the people of Israel, or from God. But insofar as you reach out to *me*, and insofar as I can separate myself from my fellow Jews, for whom I cannot speak, my broken heart pleads for your broken heart: Go in peace."

But let me hasten to add that I do not presume to judge the narrator. He was himself psychologically and spiritually *in extremis*. His anguish was almost as great as that of the young man on his deathbed. I do not know what I would have done had I, but for the grace of God, been the one to sit beside the dying man. I only know what, years later, after calm reflection and soul-searching, I think I should have done.

The events you evoke occurred in a world which was shaking on its foundations and in an atmosphere completely impregnated with crime. Under these conditions, it is not always easy, indeed it is perhaps impossible, to assign an absolute value to right and wrong: it is in the nature of crime to create situations of moral conflict, dead ends of which bargaining or compromise are the only conditions of exit; conditions which inflict yet another wound on justice and on oneself.

When an act of violence or an offence has been committed it is for ever irreparable: it is quite probable that public opinion will cry out for a sanction, a punishment, a "price" for pain; it is also possible that the price paid be useful inasmuch as it makes amends or discourages a fresh offence, but the initial offence remains and the "price" is always (even if it is "just") a new offence and a new source of pain.

This having been said, I think I can affirm that you did well, in this situation, to refuse your pardon to the dying man. You did well because it was the lesser evil: you could only have forgiven him by lying or by inflicting upon yourself a terrible moral violence. But, of course, this refusal is not the answer to everything, and it is quite easy to see why you were left with doubts: in a case like this it is impossible to decide categorically between the answers "yes" and "no"; there always remains something to be said for the other side.

In your case, as you were a Häftling, that is a predestined victim, and since, at that moment, you felt that you represented the entire Jewish people, you would have been at fault in absolving your man, and you would perhaps today be experiencing a deeper remorse than you feel at not having absolved him.

What would this pardon have meant for the dying man and for you? Probably a great deal for the former; a kind of sacralisation, a purification which would have freed his religious conscience, all too tardily aroused, from the terror of eternal punishment. But I think that for you, it would have been meaningless: certainly it would not have meant "you are guilty of no crime", nor "you committed a crime against your will or without knowing what you were doing". On your part it would have been an empty formula and consequently a lie.

I should like to add this: the figure of the SS man as portrayed in your book does not appear as fully reinstated from the moral point of view. Everything would lead one to believe that, had it not been for his fear of impending death, he would have behaved quite otherwise: he would not have repented until much later, with the downfall of Germany or perhaps never. The act of "having a Jew brought to him" seems to me at once childish and impudent. Childish because it is too reminiscent of the defenceless child who cries out for help: it is quite possible that in his mind, bent as it was by propaganda, the "Jew" was an abnormal being—half-devil, half-miracle worker, capable in any case of supernatural deeds. Did Himmler not believe something similar when he ordered the suspension of the Lager massacres, in the hope that the "Jewish International" would assist Germany in concluding a separate peace with the West?

And impudent, because once again, the Nazi was using the Jew as a tool, unaware of the danger and the shock his request must have constituted for the prisoner: his action, examined in depth, is tinged with egoism, since one detects in it an attempt to load onto another one's own anguish.

Poul Georg Lindhardt

Simon Wiesenthal's *Sunflower* tells of an experience in the war years, revived in his memory and related with the greatest skill. His book poses the question whether it is possible to grant forgiveness by proxy, as it were, for other people. In taking up a position on this problem, I must first make it clear that any judgment of mine must be on a purely literary plane. How one personally would act in such a situation is impossible to say—since nobody can express an opinion how he would behave in a situation which is purely imaginary and unreal.

One may evaluate the book both as autobiographical and as a piece of literary art, and in both cases the high quality is evident. The story is a profound and moving one, the reader is bound to be fascinated by the intensity of the drama and by the question of conscience that it raises.

Is it possible to forgive on behalf of another? No. Such forgiveness would be words without content. That is not to say it cannot produce some sort of psychological satisfaction in the mind of a person evidently anxious for forgiveness.

A young SS man—brought up as a Catholic and a Christian, but now "Nazified"—has taken part in a bestial massacre of Jews. On his deathbed he makes an opportunity to tell his story to a Jew who is living in a concentration camp in the most humiliating conditions. At the end he asks him—as a Jew and in the name of the murdered Jews—for forgiveness. He receives no reply, but the Nazi's plea never ceases to plague the Jew's conscience.

He discusses the problem with, among others, a Catholic theologian, who says he ought to have granted forgiveness, for the SS man was at least repentant, and repentance is the most important condition for absolution. As his repentance was presumably genuine, "he has earned the grace of absolution". This last remark is unsound, for "grace" cannot be earned. There is no doubt at least that the confession was in itself a relief to his soul. The theologian says reproachfully: "Before you there lay a man in the throes of death, and you refused his last request." And your reply is: "Yes, that is exactly what is worrying me." But there are requests with which one simply cannot comply. I must admit that I sympathised with the SS man, but the certainty of not being the right authority for the granting of such a request was stronger than any sympathy.

What is definitely correct is that no man in such a case can be the "right authority". I must concur with Josek the Jew when he says: "You know, when you told me of your encounter with the SS man, I was afraid at first that you had actually forgiven him. You could only have done so in the name of people who had not empowered you to forgive. What has been done to you personally, you can, if you like, forgive and forget. In that case there is nobody to whom you have to account for your actions except yourself. But, believe me, it would have been a great sin to take other people's sufferings on your conscience."

That is very truly and precisely expressed, and accords with the prayer "Forgive us our trespasses as we forgive them that trespass against us." By that the question of the possibility of forgiveness—in a case like this—is raised above all human, ethical, and moral questions, and becomes a religious question as to the possibilities of divine grace.

But what gives Wiesenthal's book its real value is the fact the conflict of conscience is not resolved and in fact can never be resolved. After the war, the demand—especially from a so-called Christian foundation—that all should be forgiven and forgotten, was made on many occasions; "Today's world demands that we should forgive even those who still provoke us by their attitude. It demands that we draw a line under the whole business, just as if nothing of consequence had ever happened." And it is not easy to evade this demand.

At this juncture I should like to say that the death of the SS man was in fact eased, and not only because he was able to tell his story. But I must certainly dispute any comparison between "easement" and "forgiveness". Nobody need repent having eased another's death, but nobody is allowed to put himself in God's place, or feel guilt because he can never take God's place. The knowledge that the gnawing question will always gnaw is a sign that one is conscious of having no control of "grace", and also that there exists a partnership in guilt between him who asks for forgiveness and him who refuses it. A conflict of conscience which can be resolved is a mere quibble. *The Sunflower* does not concern itself with that problem, but only with the sufferings of those who "have lived through those terrible times and must suffer them over and over again in their thoughts".

Salvador de Madariaga

You ask my opinion on actions of people other than myself. I am honoured by your confidence but it imposes a burden on me. It makes me call to mind the precept laid down in the gospel: "Do not judge, and you will not be judged yourselves". I have, I admit, always regretted the second part of this rule. "Do not judge" would have sufficed me.

It is not that I intend thereby to abolish all the human mind's tendencies to judge things; but more precisely that I aspire after curbing any inclination to judge people. For there is in the human being a deep dimension which escapes the powers of judgment of any other human being. The world is a multiplicity of mutually inexplicable beings.

If then I undertake to communicate to you a few reflections on your case it is in order that I might put before you what, to the best of my belief, my study of it revealed to me concerning the moments of a human being placed by fate in an extremely abnormal situation, undergoing psychological tension of fearful intensity and called by his own sensitivity to come back to this situation when this tension has, whilst still subsisting, become less unbearable. If my exposition of these facts inevitably involves a certain degree of judgment, it is in no way a case of passing a sentence. I decline to answer the question, "was I right or wrong?"

Not only do I feel myself to be insufficiently outside and above events to do so, but I also consider that, whereas deeds actually performed exist, deeds conceived in theory do not; thus I cannot see what possible sense there could be in a sentence based on the judgment of a theoretically conceived action: "Should a man who was master of his thoughts and emotions have forgiven?" when the actual deed is so different.

I shall begin by remarking that when you were brought to the bedside of the dying man, you yourself were not in a normal state. Your psychological and moral sufferings had deprived you of the liberty and vitality of mind necessary to face up to a situation which, even for someone in a normal state, would have been almost too tense to bear. You left without answering. That is to say, you mustered up enough energy to do nothing, but no more. An initial explanation of your action may be sought then at the "energetic" level, as it were.

But I think I have an inkling of another explanation which, to my way of thinking, would reveal the very essence of your action, the essence even of that aftertaste of rejection, discordance and remorse which haunts you and does you honour. I think that at the root of all these motives, feelings, actions and inhibitions lies none other than a tension between the universal man and the tribal man in you.

This tension is at work in all of us. I have depicted it as a system of forces of which one is vertical and the other horizontal: the tribal man (Spanish, German, Jewish), is horizontal. I mean by this that the individual is free to aspire towards the highest ideals and to feel himself universal in so far as he can resist the collective and gregarious forces which bind him to the group and keep him there.

Well, it so happens that the Jewish people occupies a unique place in history from this point of view, for its horizontal forces show themselves to be of unparalleled strength and of such a kind that they have enabled it to survive throughout centuries without land or country in which to take root.

This feature of the Jewish people is the source of its magnificent strength and of the persecutions it has undergone and which make of it one of the most creative peoples of humanity.

It is in the light of these considerations that I see your dramatic experience. It is determined by a tension between universal and tribal man. The one would have forgiven; the other forbade it. Gregarious pressure goes to work through Arthur and Josek. The reading of this episode explains certain passages in the account, such as the entire episode written around Bolek and notably this sentence; "I must admit that I felt some pity for this young man, but the awareness that the granting of his request lay entirely outside my jurisdiction was stronger than any feelings of pity I might have had."

This image borrowed from judicial procedure throws light upon the essential root of the problem, showing that this sentence could equally have been written: "The man in me would have forgiven, but the Jew in me steeled himself against it."

That this tension remains alive is shown by your anxiety, by your account, by all your activities around the scene. It is also this tension which prevents you from seeing Karl as he was, whilst your loyalty permits the reader to see him as he was through the pages of your book. Your very last line confirms, it seems to me, my analysis. "I know that many will understand and approve of my attitude towards the dying SS man. But I know that just as many others will condemn me for not easing the last moments of a repentant murderer."

I do not think one can call Karl a murderer. That the war unbridled in many Nazis a natural tendency to murder is quite probable. But this was not so in Karl's case. He was a young man corrupted by his tribal surroundings before his universal being, supported by his family circle, was able to put up any resistance to these influences. He committed atrocious crimes as do so many unfortunates, and as you and I could have committed them had Heaven not protected us from forces greater than ourselves. But even if you reject this view, the fact still remains that on this bed there lay a dying man freed by death from his sinister tribal forces. The tribal man in you writes "repentant murderer". The universal man in you saw in him a dying man. It was the tribal man that shut your mouth and guided your steps to the door. And that is why Karl died taking your peace of mind with him.

I have of course given much thought to the question you ask but without reaching a solution with which I was entirely satisfied.

I am almost certain on the one hand that, had I found myself in your place beside this dying man, I should have spoken the words of forgiveness which alone could set his mind at rest in his last moments.

On the other hand, however, after further consideration, I am brought to ask myself whether such words had or could have any value. For this to be so in that particular situation I should in fact have had to assume the right to speak for the countless victims of these crimes. Well, obviously I did not have this right, nor was I endowed with the standing which alone could have given my words any real weight. Thus the apparent pardon which I would have granted that SS man would have been, if I may say so, a lie. It would simply have been the expression of a movement of pity and, at an even deeper level, one might say that it could have been explained by what was actually a somewhat egoistic endeavour to avoid having to torment myself afterwards by thinking of the entreaty which, hypothetically, I would have left unanswered.

I think then, all things being taken into consideration, that you can in no way be blamed for having remained silent. Perhaps it was your duty to do so, and I would add, an extremely cruel duty, since you had to resist the temptation of giving a dying man the peace of mind he was thirsting for.

But, as I said at the beginning of my letter, I am not satisfied with this solution because, in spite of everything, it is terrible to think that in this case repentance went completely unabsolved.

I shall end by saying that this is one of those countless instances where we must recognise that the only decisive answer lies beyond us and that it can be formulated only in the hereafter.

Herbert Marcuse

I think I would have acted the way you did, that is to say, refused the request of the dying SS man. It always seemed to me inhuman and a travesty of justice if the executioner asked the victim to forgive. One cannot, and should not go around happily killing and torturing and then, when the moment has come, simply ask, and receive, forgiveness. In my view, this perpetuates the crime.

By the way, the question transcends the Jewish problem. As a member of the National Liberation Front, would one forgive a Marine sergeant the killing and torturing of one's friends, wife, children? Is anyone justified, entitled to forgive?

I still remember the traumatic shock I had when I read that, after the assassination of Rathenau, his mother went to the assassin's mother and comforted her!

I believe that the easy forgiving of such crimes perpetuates the very evil it wants to alleviate.

Jacques Maritain

I do not condemn you for having left without forgiving Karl but, like Bolek, I think it would have been *better* to forgive him, putting yourself for a moment in the place of the priest who would have heard his confession and saying to him for example: "I could forgive you only for any wrong you might have done to me personally. How, though, could I, in their name, forgive you for the atrocities you committed against others? What you have done is, humanly speaking, unforgivable. But *in the name of your God*, yes, I forgive you."

I think you are still in a position to perform this act of charity now, in prayer and before God (all moments of time being present in divine eternity), and that this will put your conscience at rest.

Martin E. Marty

"What would I have done?"

The author's final question is designed to haunt. The word that leaps, nags, and accuses is "I." Here there is no thought of categorical imperatives or universal principles. What would *I* have done? Ortega reminds us: "I am I and my circumstances." My circumstances are unimaginably different from his. It is difficult, then, to imagine an answer to his question.

Almost two thousand years after the early Christians were martyred by the Romans we Christian children were taught to prepare ourselves. We, too, might be called upon to witness even unto death. Strange how powerful a story can remain for two millennia. So it shall be with the recall of the Holocaust for the descendants of Jews. Astute teachers would remind us that martyrdoms continued. Even as we sat in school, Christians were dying for their faith in Russia, Germany, and elsewhere. At the time I was in third grade Dietrich Bonhoeffer, a Christian who was later to die in one of Hitler's camps, was writing a book on discipleship. Its first line told us that when Jesus Christ calls a man he calls him to die.

Without doubt I prepared myself intellectually as a child for such discipleship. I am not sure that if my circumstances called me to such extremes I would be ready. I, who cower in the dentist's chair and shrink from minor pain—would I be able to stand torture? I, who have been trained or who have trained myself to look past or to overlook injustices and suffering every day—would I be ready to witness? "What would I have done?" I do not know. But the author's question pursues beyond that first evasion.

"What would I have done?" becomes "What *should* I have done?" But to answer that question would identify me again with the author and his circumstances, something that is impossible for me to do. Even the author's fellow prisoners do not satisfy him with the counsel they offer. Were I to respond directly, it would be necessary for me to get almost as close as they, to share the experience of the author's people. But is there then a single prescription, a single "ought" or "should?" His committee of counselors some- times seems to imply that there is. To act one way would be to deny the Jewish people. To act another way would be to affirm them. I prefer his lifelong uncertainty to their counsel. To say that all persons in a people must act a specific way is to routinize them, to program them, to deprive them of elements of their humanity.

Viktor Frankl, the psychiatrist who survived the death camps, has pondered the question of exceptionality there and thenceforth. Why did some prisoners who knew they were to die that day still spread comfort and share bread? He could not answer, but he did note that they demonstrated that one freedom cannot be taken away: the freedom to choose one's own attitude in the face of any circumstance. The author chose the attitude of perplexity and bemusement. He chose to let himself be haunted all his life. Who is to say that his choice is inferior to the counselors', for they were more sure of themselves and the impact of peoplehood.

Speaking of peoplehood and circumstances, one more thing must be said. I am a Christian, and I hear the question framed against Wiesenthal's experience. So it sounds like this: "What would/should a Jew have done?" I cannot imagine being asked to this symposium except for the fact that I am a Christian. So I hear, "What does a Christian say?" And in that way of stating it I can only respond with silence. Non-Jews and perhaps especially Christians should not give advice about Holocaust experience to its heirs for the next two thousand years. And then we shall have nothing to say.

This does not mean that the Holocaust has to be set apart qualitatively from the experience of all other genocides and victimizations in history. To do so would be to dishonor innocent sufferers elsewhere. Modern Armenians, tribesmen in Africa, peoples of the Asian subcontinent have all experienced hatreds and madnesses as have the Jews. They may appear on statistically smaller scales, but I do not begin to comprehend the Holocaust if I say that others' suffering was less meaningful or less valid. But it happens that the Holocaust is webbed into "our" history—Western and Western religious history. This circumstance impels silence. Cheap instant advice from a Christian would trivialize the lives and deaths of millions.

Forget, then, the author's circumstance and keep the

essence of his question for me. Is there any kind of situation in which the offense is so gross and enormous that I should withhold forgiveness in the face of what appears to be true penitence? My answer would be that in every circumstance that I can picture, more value would grow out of forgiveness than out of its withholding. But I must ask what am I afraid of or concerned about, and what is it that causes me to hem and hedge, to shuffle and clear my throat, to be suspicious of that answer?

First, I am afraid of "cheap grace," as were *The Sunflower* people. W. H. Auden's Herod parodies a version of Christian forgiveness. He sees every corner newsboy remarking that he likes to commit sins and God likes to forgive them so the world is admirably arranged. No. Nothing should happen that would let haters or murderers off the hook by assuring them that grace is readily available. The author's silence in that hospital room was a guard against the cheapening of grace.

A second fear: crimes against a people will be taken less seriously if individual persons start forgiving in their name. The question is here raised, then, whether latter-day Germans who do express repentance should be allowed to feel forgiven. Here I must raise the question whether it is always valuable to prolong a people's sense of guilt. As a white, they tell me that I must always feel guilty and grovel over what whites in the American past did when they killed Indians and enslaved blacks. And, to a measure, I do. But I have sufficient guilt for my own faults in relation to the heirs of the Indians and blacks, and to many other people. Is there not a limit to the good that can be achieved by my groveling, my self-hate, my loss of pride in the positive features of my heritages? Did not Nazism in part grow out of such negative and resentful views? Must I not also be given a means for retrieving from a people's history some moments, models, motifs that can give dignity and nobility to a history?

The third reason for pause: if grace be cheap and splattered at random, will we not soon forget to tell the story? Theodor Adorno and Alexander Solzhenitsyn have both reminded us that to forget to tell the story is to deprive past sufferers of the meaning of their act. But there are many ways to tell the story. Wiesenthal's ambivalence stays in our mind because he has taken pains to tell us of it. So would other attitudes, if there be storytellers to broadcast them.

We do not want cheap grace, a casual people, or a forgotten victim. What do we want? I am on a search for grace in the world. While my colleagues write on the phenomenology of evil or of the will, I want to see what grace feels like. As a Christian I am told that God is a gracious Other, but I also need and need to be a gracious brother. Gracelessness helps produce totalitarianisms as much as cheap grace might. If there is to be grace, it must be mediated through people. We have to see potentials in the lives of even the worst people, have to see that it is we who can dam the flow of grace. I do not for a moment claim that this insight is mine because I am a Christian; phenomenologically speaking, such a concept of grace is shared by people of many faiths and of no clear faith. Reportorially, it often has not been visible on Christian soil. But that does not mean that a turn cannot now be taken.

If I forgive in the face of true repentance and new resolve, I am free. Wiesenthal successfully works on the basis of his uncertainty; it motivates him. But I can let my being haunted preoccupy me so that I do not notice "the other." Forgiving and being forgiven are experiences that allow me to be free for a new day. I cannot say that I would be more free or more creative than is Wiesenthal. That is because I cannot say what he should have done but only what I would like to think I would want to do.

John M. Oesterreicher

Man is meant to walk the earth, not as a deaf-mute but as one able to ask questions and search for answers. It is, therefore, not surprising that a story of the most fateful decisions in the lives of two agonized men ends with a question. But is it legitimate for an author to ask his reader what he would have done, had he been in his protagonist's stead? Why does he wish to know if I or, for that matter, any other reader would have acted as he did? Would I, too, have remained mute in the presence of a dying man who begged me to help him leave this world in peace, or would I have comforted him? Would I, too, have denied mercy to a Nazi murderer, or would I have taken his pleading hand and, with him, asked for God's forgiveness? Would I have done the latter, had I myself gone through the hell our protagonist had endured?

I do not pretend to such insight. Thus I will not even attempt an answer lest I be chastened by the Zanser Rebbe. We are told that at one time Rabbi Hayyim wished to have a glimpse of men's hearts and test their opinions of themselves. He called some passersby into his house and asked each one: "Suppose you found a purse full of gold pieces, would you return it to its rightful owner?" "Without doubt. I would do so right away provided, of course, I knew who the owner was," the first one answered. "Fool," said the rabbi. Turning to another with the same question, he was told: "Of course not. I am not so stupid as to let a windfall like this out of my hands." "You scoundrel," the rabbi exclaimed. A third man, free of delusion and malice, replied: "How can I possibly know, rabbi, what I would be like then? Would I be able to conquer the evil inclination? Or would the evil urge overcome me and make me take what belongs to another? I do not know. But if the Holy One, blessed be He, strengthened me against the evil inclination, I would restore the find." "Your words are beautiful," the Zanser Rebbe marvelled, "you are wise indeed."

Far be it from me to claim such wisdom for myself. Although striving for it, I must forego the opportunity of writing my own story, as it were. As I put down these words, I wonder whether I have fully understood the narrator of our story. I wonder if the question as printed does not hide another, more alarming one. As I see it, the narrator—the sound of his request notwithstanding—really wants us, his readers, to approve his decision or, failing such justification, condemn it. Conversations like the one the narrator has with Bolek, the Polish seminarian whose faith remains unbroken, despite the cruelties he witnessed and the tortures he himself endured, seem to confirm this view (see pp. 81-83). A man of profound moral concern, he may—so it seems to me—prefer to have his attitude condemned than dismissed as unimportant.

Yet, sitting in the comfort and safety of my home, far from the pains and threats that were the hourly fare of concentration camp "dwellers," I cannot possibly sit in judgment over their reactions. The KZ victim described in these pages seems paralyzed in mind and will. A "natural" reaction to the dying man's plea might have been: "How dare you ask forgiveness, after all the horrors you and your ilk have heaped on my people? You want to die, your soul bathed in tranquility—How about my kinsmen who are not allowed to die or, for a single minute, live in peace? For years you Nazis considered us vermin, subhuman beings; now, suddenly, you think that I, a subhuman Jew, can save you. Call on your Führer, not on me." This is how he might have spoken; instead he is stunned, numb, unable to utter words of pity or anger. Hence I dare neither applaud nor denounce his inaction.

This does not mean that I am indifferent, that I do not wish the prisoner had thrown off the chains his anguish had forged and mounted to the heights of mercy. There is enough evidence in the story that our narrator thinks of forgiveness as the virtue, not of weaklings, but of the inwardly strong. The one who pardons rises above the desire for revenge; the mechanics of soul and history; the law of savagery and rule of murderous instincts the Nazi sought to enthrone; most of all, above the human condition ever-exposed to sin and death.

In reconciling one human being to another, or man to God, the one who forgives restores, even though it may seem only on a small scale, the integrity of being. "Only on a small scale" implies a surface view, referring as it does to appearance; at their deepest reality, all events exist on a great, a world scale. Viewed philosophically, the whole is present in all its parts. Thus it can be said that the history of each person—undoubtedly *part* of world history—*is* world history. In other words, anything a man or woman does, even in secret, touches, more than that, shapes the whole of mankind.

When in that isolated hospital room a faceless SS man and a defaced Jew met in subtle combat, their meeting may have seemed irrelevant to the world outside, without bearing on the life of other people. Throughout these pages, our protagonist tries hard to convince himself that, as an individual Jew, he had no power to forgive sins committed against other Jews—indeed, his entire people. He is at pains to resist even the possibility that the confrontation between him, an impotent but, for an instant, omnipotent Jew, and a Nazi, once in control of life and death, but now helpless, was more than a meeting between two unrelated individuals. Yet, as he demurs, he somehow realizes that in that death chamber representatives of two hostile worlds were yet seeking one another. He realizes that here was a pregnant moment he missed. Hence, among other things, his pointless visit to the dead man's mother; his telling and retelling of the story.

To no other creature but man, made in God's image, has it been granted to forgive. Faculties, however, are given in order to be used. It is not only the New Testament but also the Jewish tradition, before and afterwards, which proclaims the grandeur of man's power to pardon and moves him to exercise it. One of Israel's proverbs (ca. fifth century B.C.) urges: "If your enemy is hungry, give him bread to eat; if he is thirsty, give him water to drink" (Proverbs 25:21). Centuries later, Ben Sirach (ca. 180 B.C.) prods: "Forgive your neighbor his wrongdoing" (Ben Sirach 28:2).

This admonition may well have been the basis for the petition in the Lord's Prayer: "Forgive us our sins, as we forgive those who have sinned against us" (Matthew 6:12).

Rabbi Gamaliel II (ca. 100 A.D.) is credited with saying, as long as we show mercy to others, God will be merciful to us; if we do not, He will not turn in mercy to us either (J. Baba Kamma VIII). Rabbi Abbahu, a teacher about 300 A.D., counsels that a person should always strive to be of the persecuted rather than of the persecutors (Baba Kamma 93a).

Christian proclamation and Jewish tradition do not merely admonish us to forgive others whenever they repent of their wrongdoing; both are filled with the promise and actuality of God's forbearance and pardon. One of the most moving revelations of the Lord's ways with men is given through Moses at Mt. Sinai: "The Lord, the Lord, a God compassionate and gracious, long-suffering, ever constant and true . . . , forgiving iniquity, rebellion, and sin . . ." (Exodus 34:6-7). Could it be that ultimately the protagonist could not forgive because he had lost faith in the God of Israel?

To repent and to forgive are not arrogant struggles to change the course of events, vain attempts to undo what has been done; rather are they daring, loving ventures to offer new meaning to the "dead" and deadly past. In doing so, these acts give a new direction to history. But can there be meaning, a new creative beginning, without God? Can a man or woman wish to give new significance to the past if he or she is convinced that the present, that all life is bare of it, that meaning is but an idle dream begotten by human wretchedness?

As I read the story, it is—whatever the author's intention—basically, not about forgiveness, but about faith. The primary problem, then, is not whether or not its protagonist ought to have forgiven a repentant murderer of Jews who begged him to do so, but whether after the Holocaust a Jew or a Christian can still believe in God, whether they can still say: "Give thanks to the Lord, for He is good, His covenant love endures forever" (Psalms 118:1)

Early in the story we are told that many inside the camp and outside were overtaken by doubt and unbelief. "It is impossible to believe anything in a world that has ceased to regard man as man," the narrator maintains. If one is shown again and again, he continues, "that one is no longer a man, so one begins to doubt, one begins to cease to believe in a world order in which God has a definite place. One really begins to think that God is on leave. Otherwise the present state of things wouldn't be possible. God must be away. And He has no deputy" (p. 14f).

I do not know what the belief in "a world order in which God has a definite place" is called; it certainly is not belief in the living God, the God of Abraham, Isaac, and Jacob. The God who is an ocean of Being, infinite Life, the all-pervading Spirit is not like a police chief who from his office controls a city, sending his flying squads to every trouble spot so that order will be restored. According to Scripture, man is addressed by God and bidden to respond; among all the creatures he is the one to whom God has spoken and who must answer with his whole existence.

Our prayers, our actions, our lives are a dialogue with Him, a meeting, an exchange in which—here I depart from Buber's thought—God is I *and* Thou, in which man, too, is an I and a Thou. Once one has seen reality in this light, one cannot possibly say that "God has no deputy." The deepest meaning of the biblical vision of human beings as God's image and likeness is that they are His partners and thus charged to act as His representatives at all times. In a church in Muenster, Germany, hangs a cross, the body of the Crucified armless; during the war the arms had been torn off by bombs. Beneath this mutilated figure stand the words: "God has no other hands but yours."

With all His strength, Jesus shouted on the cross: "My God, my God, why have you forsaken me?" (Matthew 27:46). The words are originally those of the innocent sufferer who pours out his heart in the twenty-second Psalm. On Jesus' lips the cry bespeaks His own agony but in and with Him scream all the tormented of this earth. They have found in Him their advocate. The cry has been called the most desperate utterance in Scripture, but it is not. Even though the words rise from the abyss of a felt abandonment, they are addressed to the Father, with humble trust.

The whole biblical tradition follows this route. From Abraham to Job, from various psalmists to Jeremiah, believers complain, plead, or argue with the Lord, they even take Him to task, but it is always to the Lord they turn, not to themselves. The prophet, for instance, cries out:

> O Lord, I will dispute with you, for you are just;
>   Yes, I will plead my case before you.
> Why do the wicked prosper
>   and traitors live at ease? . . .
> How long must the earth mourn
>   and its green grass wither?
>
> (Jeremiah 12:1, 4)

What a different way of de-crying, even denouncing God's silence while evil seems to rule the world than our narrator's impersonal "God is on leave," to which one of his comrades replies, with supposedly ingenuous humor: "Tell me when He gets back" (p. 15).

Talk about the absent God is quite frequent today; in fact, it is "in." My heart goes out to, and trembles with, the sufferer who in his deep anguish even utters blasphemies. Yet, my heart draws back from those—particularly Christians—who turn torment (mostly someone else's) into theological trash and a piece of self-aggrandizement. Today's faddists, who think themselves brave when they accuse God of Satanism, for instance, claim one of the Hasidic masters, Rabbi Levi Yitzhak of Berditchev (1740-1809), as their "patron saint." But wrongly.

It was generally in the midst of one of the services that Rabbi Levi Yitzhak turned to God and pleaded, even demanded that He take Israel out of her misery. Buber says of him: "He confronted [God] not only as the passionate intercessor for Israel, he took him to account, made demands on him, and even ventured to hurl threats—a bitter and sublime jest which would have been blasphemy in another, but was irreproachable coming from the lips of this unique character." So great was Rabbi Levi Yitzhak's love of God that he, plaintiff and prosecutor, used to sing:

> Where I wander—You!
> Where I ponder—You!
> Only You, You again, always You!
> You! You! You! . . .
>
> Sky is You! Earth is You!
> You above! You below!
> In every trend, at every end,
> Only You, You again, always You!
> You! You! You!

In Israel's name, the ancient rabbis lament the devastation of the Holy City and the destruction of the Temple in 70 A.D., though they fully acknowledge the sins of the generation that brought about Jerusalem's ruin. A special current of the Jewish tradition, however, has the Lord Himself grieve over the City's downfall, while mindful of the sins of His children that "forced" Him to let both City and Temple be knocked into rubble. Thus it is said, His eyes and heart are there, at all times; He roars like a lion bewailing the disaster He had to bring on them; He weeps inconsolably, "two great hot tears falling down from the throne of Heaven into the depth of the sea." In short, He suffers when Israel suffers.

In the Christian tradition, the outstretched arms of Jesus nailed to the cross tell of God's embrace of every man and woman in their misery. He can even say: "Once I am lifted up from the earth I will draw all men to myself" (John 12:32). As redeemer, Jesus had to "become like His brethren in every way" (Hebrews 2:17), suffer death, share our fears and pain.

The God of Israel and Father of Jesus Christ is thus not a kind of understudy or heavenly minuteman, He is the One who lives and suffers with His own. Thus the question that Auschwitz and other substations of hell pose is not: How can a Jew or Christian still believe in the God of righteousness and compassion? It is rather: How can anyone, remembering the Holocaust, continue to live and not believe in Him?

Cynthia Ozick

NOTES TOWARD A MEDITATION ON "FORGIVENESS"

1. *The uses of Jesus*

The SS man had a Catholic education. As a boy he was a "server in the church." Should not a Christian education make it impossible for a child to grow up to be an SS man? Should not a sentence like "The SS man had a Catholic education" be so thoroughly a contradiction of its own terms that the words come out jabberwocky?

The words do not come out jabberwocky; the SS man *did* have a Christian education.

Does the habit, inculcated in infancy, of worshiping a

Master—a Master depicted in human form yet seen to be omnipotent—make it easy to accept a Führer?

2. *The sources of pity*

Pity is not "felt," as if by instinct or reflex. Pity is taught. But what is the original source of pity? What teaches it? The Second Commandment—the one against idols.

Every idol is a shadow of Moloch, demanding human flesh to feed on. The deeper the devotion to the idol, the more pitiless in tossing it its meal will be the devotee. The Commandment against idols is above all a Commandment against victimization, and in behalf of pity.

Moloch springs up wherever the Second Commandment is silenced. In the absence of the Second Commandment, the hunt for victims begins.

The Second Commandment is more explicit than the Sixth, which tells us simply that we must not kill; the Second Commandment tells us we must resist especially that killing which serves our belief.

In Germany, did the Church say, "Hitler is Moloch"?

Moloch's appetite for victims cannot be stemmed. Begin by feeding it only Jews, and in the end it will eat even the little boys who are servers in their church.

There are no innocent idols. Every idol suppresses human pity. That is what it is made for.

3. *Vengeance and forgiveness*

Is the morally obsessed human being more drawn to vengeance or to forgiveness?

What is vengeance, what is forgiveness?

Often we are asked to think this way: vengeance brutalizes, forgiveness refines.

But the opposite can be true. The rabbis said, "Whoever is

merciful to the cruel will end by being indifferent to the innocent." Forgiveness can brutalize.

You will object, "Only if it seems to condone. But forgiveness does not condone or excuse. It allows for redemption, for a clean slate, a fresh start; it encourages beginning again. Forgiveness permits renewal."

Only if there is a next time. "I forgive you," we say to the child who has muddied the carpet, "but next time don't do it again." Next time she will leave the muddy boots outside the door; forgiveness, with its enlarging capacities, will have taught her. Forgiveness is an effective teacher. Meanwhile, the spots can be washed away.

But murder is irrevocable. Murder is irreversible. With murder there is no "next time." Even if forgiveness restrains one from perpetrating a new batch of corpses (and there is no historical demonstration of this in Nazi Germany), will the last batch come alive again?

There are spots forgiveness cannot wash out. Forgiveness, which permits redemption, can apply only to a condition susceptible of redemption.

You will object: "If forgiveness cannot wash away murder, neither can vengeance. If forgiveness is not redemptive, surely vengeance is less so, because vengeance requites evil with an equal evil, thereby adding to the store of evil in the world."

But that is a misunderstanding. Vengeance does not requite evil with evil; vengeance cannot requite, repay, even out, equate, redress. If it could, vengeance on a mass murderer would mean killing all the members of his family and a great fraction of his nation; and still his victims would not come alive.

What we call "vengeance" is the act of bringing public justice to evil—not by repeating the evil, not by imitating the evil, not by initiating a new evil, but by making certain never to condone the old one; never even appearing to condone it.

"Public" justice? Yes. While the evil was going on, to turn aside from it, to avoid noticing it, became complicity. And in the same way, after three or four decades have passed and the evil has entered history, to turn aside from it—to forget—again becomes complicity. Allowing the evil to slip into the collective amnesia of its own generation, or of the next generation, is tantamount to condoning it.

You will object: "Here you are, naming vengeance as public justice because it does not condone evil. But forgiveness too does not condone evil. It doesn't matter that it may sometimes appear to; the fact is it doesn't. And you have already demonstrated that there are some evils forgiveness cannot wash away. Yet now you say that vengeance, like forgiveness, neither condones nor washes away the evil. How, then, do vengeance and forgiveness differ?"

In this way: forgiveness is pitiless. It forgets the victim. It negates the right of the victim to his own life. It blurs over suffering and death. It drowns the past. It cultivates sensitiveness toward the murderer at the price of insensitiveness toward the victim.

What is always characterized as "vengeance"—which is to say, a justice that enlightens the world as to the nature of evil (and by "nature of evil" I do not mean something philosophical or metaphysical, but the exact conduct of the evildoer: what precisely was done; when and where; by whom; to whom)—this so-called vengeance is fired by the furnaces of pity. This so-called vengeance—justice in apposite dress—generates fire after fire of pity.

I forgot for a moment where I was and then I heard a buzzing sound. A bluebottle ... flew round the head of the dying [SS] man, who could not see it nor could he see me wave it away.

"Thanks," he nevertheless whispered. And for the first time I realized that I, a defenseless subhuman, had contrived to lighten the lot of an equally defenseless superman, without thinking, simply as a matter of course (p. 41).

The young man who will become Simon Wiesenthal, who will become the world's "Nazi-hunter," waves a fly from the wound of the dying Nazi "without thinking, simply as a matter of course." A hand striking out for pity. At that moment the SS man is seen as the victim of a fly.

Vengeance, only vengeance, knows pity for the victim.

You will object: "Oratory! And if he had forgiven the SS man, he would *not* have waved away the fly?"

He would not have noticed it at all. Whoever forgives the murderer blinds himself to the vastest letting of blood—how then should he see the smallest mite?

It is forgiveness that is relentless. The face of forgiveness is mild, but how stony to the slaughtered.

4. *Moral tenderness, moral responsibility*

Consider this dying SS man. Is he not unlike so many others? He, at least, shows the marks of conscience, of remorse, of sickness at his life. He is not arrogant; he is not self-justifying; he feels disgust at everything he has witnessed, he recoils from everything he has committed. He is a man at a moral turning. Ought he not to be delivered over to his death—to use the old Christian word—shriven? *He* is penitent, so many others are not—should the penitent be treated like the impenitent? Should a revived goodness, a recovered cleanliness of heart, be dealt with exactly as one would deal with the recalcitrance of an unregenerate brute?

Consider now the brute. He exults in his brutishness. Remorse never touches him; even in memory, even thirty years after those butcheries of his, he exults in them. His mind, dim for other matters, is a bright and secret screen on which he renews and replenishes these triumphs of his old lost barbaric power over the weak. He was a great man then; he was like an angel, he served in fact the Angel of Death, lives were in his hands and under his feet, his boots were on the necks of the doomed. As he never experienced regret then, so now he never dreams of wishing away the old sensations and reminders.

But the dying SS man has had twinges all along. He has, in fact, a moral temperament. He is intelligently contrite; he knows there is no way for him to atone, but he understands what atonement is, he understands the force of contrition. He is a man with a vigorous insight into his own moral nature. He is a man with a conscience.

Should not some special recognition—some softening of condemnation—be given to the man of conscience? We condemn the brute; he is a barbarian; we condemn him as we condemn every barbarian. How then can we dare to condemn the man of conscience, as if there were no difference between him and the barbarian?

We condemn the intelligent man of conscience because there *is* a difference*; because, though at heart not a savage, he allowed himself to become one, he did not resist. It was not that he lacked conscience; he smothered it. It was not that he lacked sensibility; he coarsened it. It was not that he lacked humanity; he deadened it.

*For the root of this insight I am indebted to Professor Melvin L. Plotinsky of Indiana University.

The brute runs to feed Moloch because to him Moloch is not a false god, but a Delightful True Lord, the Master who brings him exaltation. In exaltation he shovels in the babies. He has no conscience to stop him, no moral education, no moral insight. Perhaps he was never a server in his church. Does he even know what wickedness is?

The intelligent man of conscience also shovels in the babies, and it does not matter that he does it without exaltation. Conscience, education, insight—nothing stops him. He goes on shoveling. He knows what wickedness is. By now he has been shoveling for so long that he knows what Moloch is, he is intimate with Moloch. He is a morally sensitive man, and he shovels babies to glut the iron stomach of the idol.

The morally sensitive SS man goes on shoveling, and shoveling, and shoveling.

A virtuous childhood as a server in his church lies behind him; he shovels. A virtuous future as a model of remorse lies ahead of him; he shovels. He shovels and shovels, all the while possessed of a refined and meticulous moral temperament—so refined and so meticulous that it knows the holy power of forgiveness, and knows to ask for it.

I discover a quotation attributed to Hannah Arendt: "The only antidote to the irreversibility of history is the faculty of forgiveness." Jabberwocky at last. She is the greatest moral philosopher of the age, but even she cannot make a Lazarus of history.

Graham Greene explains the Catholic idea of hell—no longer that medieval site of endless conflagration; instead, an eternal separation from God.

Let the SS man die unshriven.

Let him go to hell.

Sooner the fly to God than he.

James William Parkes

It is a moving, a very moving story. It would require a quite shocking lack of sensitivity for anyone to criticise the actions and reactions of the three leading Jewish figures in the story, Arthur, Josek and the author. I find that the nobility with which the author listened to the dying boy, and afterwards to his mother is more than most of us could achieve. To me the whole story goes much deeper than the attempts of either Ulrich Simon or Ignaz Maybaum to reconcile belief in a benevolent and intelligent Creator with the facts of the Holocaust. In the confrontation of the Jewish concentration camp inmate with the dying and repentant SS boy, we are face to face not only with the unity of humanity—as the author realises—but the unity of life this side of, and beyond, physical death.

Both Judaism and Christianity hold similar views of the place of repentance in the destiny of man. Sincere repentance earns the forgiveness of God; but where the sin repented of has been against a fellow man, more than repentance is needed. The man can show his repentance only in making every effort to atone for the wrong which he has done. Judaism states this explicitly in its teaching about the Day of Atonement. Christianity has the saying of Jesus (Matt. V: 23) "If thou bring thine offering to the altar and thou remember there that thy brother has ought against thee, leave thy offering there before the altar, and go, first be reconciled to thy brother, and then come and bring thine offering".

But what if the sin against the brother brought about his death? How is atonement to be made? For Josek is right in saying that it is the wronged alone who can forgive the wrong.

191

The Sunflower has brought into the open a need which I have long felt, and one which is common to both Jews and Christians, though the official interpreters of both faiths offer no help to resolve it. Those who do not believe in a Creator can legitimately believe that there is nothing human which survives bodily death. But the problem is different for those who not only believe in a Creator, but believe also, as do Jews and Christians, that He is intelligent, responsible, and benevolent in His attitude to His creation. If these adjectives, however inadequate they be, really apply to Him, then I do not see how He can face the responsibility of having endowed His creation with free will *except* on the basis that He will bring it finally to the perfection for which He designed it. And that is impossible if the span of human life is limited to the experience we pass through between physical birth and physical death. I think it is also impossible unless the Creator possesses a moral certainty that he will redeem his whole creation. I have long ceased to believe in a final division of the sheep from the goats, especially a division (such as I was taught in my youth) which took place at the moment of death.

I am absolutely convinced that the young Nazi, in his repentance, goes into the next life seeking those whom he so terribly wronged, and seeking those whom, very likely without repentance, wrought the wrong with him. That alone to me makes sense of the world as the work of a Creator such as I have described. That alone reconciles on the one hand the infinite beauty and richness of the creation and, on the other, the immeasurable horror of evil of which the Holocaust is certainly the most appalling example.

Men who are dying expect special consideration. Often enough, they are badly frightened and deeply unhappy. To ask absolution for one's sins when near death is a perfectly normal human reflex. What is completely unusual about Simon Wiesenthal's book, *The Sunflower*, is that a dying SS man should have sought absolution from people whom he had helped to persecute. This, obviously, poses a problem of immense complexity.

First, there is the problem of the SS man's conscience. If he wished merely to "confess", he could have done so to a priest of his own religion. He could have asked God's forgiveness and he would, presumably, have received the standard answer that God's compassion is infinite, whenever repentance is real. Anyone who has fought on the battlefield knows that repentance, in the face of danger, seems real enough. Men under fire who have never prayed before, pray and promise "to be good" in the future—if God will oblige by rescuing them from impending death. The certainty, rather than the mere possibility of death can only reinforce the plea for mercy. This is what Wiesenthal's SS man was after.

For the Jew to whom he made his plea the problem was totally different. The Jew was facing death every day that he remained alive. He knew that the very most that he could achieve for himself would be to face death bravely and to maintain his faith in his own identity up to the end. Had I been such a Jew I would have been affronted by the SS man's plea. I would have regarded it as an attempt to seek a cheap and easy "way out", and the gift of a few belongings as a histrionic, mock-sentimental gesture.

A persecuted Jew could only forgive wrongs done to him

personally; he could not possibly forgive genocide. I find the idea of a mock-forgiveness of a man who had helped to burn women and children alive repellent, and I cannot see how it could be other than mock-forgiveness, granted simply because a man happened to be dying. To forgive this one SS man would mean, by implication, to forgive every other SS man who murdered, on his deathbed.

The SS man should have been asking forgiveness of God, and not of man. He had sinned against the principles of humanity far more than he had sinned against a handful of doomed human beings. This was a matter between him and his Creator, not between him and a single, stray Jew picked out of a random working-party and forced to listen to his "confession".

Should the Jew have told him this? It would be too much to expect of a badgered, brutalised concentration-camp inmate to play the role of a philosopher. Nor could he possibly act as father-confessor. He showed, in any case, remarkable restraint in listening to the SS man's terrible story without expressing his horror and hatred of such bestial cruelty. By walking out of the room without a word, he did the most sensible, the most logical, basically the most decent thing possible.

Luise Rinser

The fact that an experience of twenty-seven years ago still disquiets your conscience may be considered in itself a clear answer to your question as to whether your action in refusing forgiveness was right or wrong. One might indeed ask why or for what purpose you are seeking the opinions of other people? Unless you are expecting nothing other than a soothing acknowledgement that you acted rightly. But I cannot suppose that your question is prompted by any such dishonesty, nor that you think your problem capable of a simple answer. It is in fact not capable of any easy or immediate solution. You know that yourself. If I were now to say what was my immediate reaction, i.e., that you did wrong, I should be setting myself up as a judge over you and should be doing exactly what you yourself did long ago and what you wish you had never done, namely act as judge, set yourself up as judge over another human being. The Bible says: "Judge not, that you be not judged." True I differentiate my judging from yours in that you have time to make reparation, but the young man whom you judged had not. And that is a great difference.

But the problem is not so simple as all that. The specific difficulty is the fact that you were not asked to forgive something which had been done to you personally, but something which had been done to your people. It was not a simple confrontation of two persons, but between the representatives of two groups of people, who were connected by the unequivocal relationship of an evildoer and an innocent and defenceless victim.

I can very well imagine that you could have forgiven the young man if he had inflicted a severe wound on you—but on you alone—or had killed a near relative of yours. From my knowledge of Jews I can say that the lengthy, painful experiences of your people have made the individual Jew ready to understand and forgive. Shylock is not a typical Jew, nor indeed is Nathan.

If that young man had done you a personal injury and you had refused him your forgiveness, I would have had to say that your guilt was as great as his, because he had acted in ignorance and you were acting with your eyes open. You could not be forgiven, because you had refused to forgive.

But this case is one in which the great wrong was committed by one group of people against another, and it is questionable whether you as an individual were in any way authorised to forgive. You yourself recognised the position when you said, "I found myself obliged to refuse him pardon." What forced your refusal—I underline this again—was the realisation that an individual Jew could not forgive what had been done to Jewry.

I found myself confronted with this question of forgiveness after the end of the war. In 1944 former friends of mine had denounced me. I was arrested, and at the People's Court in Berlin proceedings were taken against me which at that time could only end with a death sentence. I was saved by the end of the war. In 1945 I could have handed over my denunciators to the Americans. Later I could have prevented them from returning to their former occupations (primary school teachers). But I did nothing of the kind. Why not? When later my former friends sent me a letter begging my pardon, I replied: "You are making excuses to me. That is quite unnecessary and senseless. Unnecessary, since, for me personally, the sufferings in prison were far surpassed by the spiritual gains of that period. Your excuses have no point, for they are too late and come from an unclean source. Your faith in Hitler collapsed at the moment when National Socialism collapsed. Your change of mind is not the recognition of the lies, malice, folly, and inhumanity of that regime, but merely your bitter experiences when it perished . . . No, I do not accept your excuses, what I can never forget or forgive is the hatred which lay in your eyes when we were confronted by the security service at Berchtesgaden. It was not you, it was the madness that had taken possession of you, just as it possessed so many others. But now let us make an end of hatred, blood and death. What we need, we the survivors who must have learnt

something from these terrible years, is peace and humanity."
(From my prison memories, first published in 1946.)

You see: I have forgiven and not forgiven. What my two
friends did to *me* I have forgiven, in the sense that I abandoned
any thought of revenge and was ready to render them any sort
of assistance had they asked me for it. But I did *not* forgive
them for declaring their solidarity with the followers of a
stupid and wicked ideology, which caused the deaths of millions of people. I am accustomed, as free from prejudice as
possible, to take into account and even to understand all the
motives which lead to an action or an attitude, but I realise
that there are limits to understanding, forgetting and forgiving. The limit is where somebody does something, not to me
but to others. In saying this I seem to approve unreservedly
your refusal to pardon.

And yet this is not the final answer to your question. The
final answer lies in a consideration of the special situation in
which you found yourself at the time. The SS man, you say,
was young. From this one can deduce that, led astray by Nazi
ideology (he knew nothing except Nazi propoganda) he
thought he was acting rightly when he killed Jews. In moral
theology (and not in Christian theology only) there is right in
a mistaken conscience. It is thinkable, therefore, that the
young man was subjectively guiltless until the moment in
which he became conscious of his guilt through some occurrence or other which you do not mention. That he should
become conscious of his guilt was in itself a pardon. And
thereupon he asked your forgiveness for that which he had
done to your brothers and sisters in his state of ignorance. He
could not ask the dead for forgiveness, nor all living Jews. He
had you alone. For him you were simply *the* Jew. In his
thoughts you were authorised to forgive. The whole guilt-
complex was laid on both of you, and you, the Jew, were

called upon to act in exemplary fashion. Were you authorised by your people *not* to forgive? No. Perhaps you acted against the wish of the dead Jews. I hope that those dead Jews will grant you "extenuating circumstances" in view of the difficulty of the case. Your dead folk will know whether at that moment you acted with mental clarity and ethical honesty, or whether you were blinded by hate (that too might be understandable). But I shudder at the thought that you let that *repentant* young man go to his death without a word of forgiveness. I must admit that you found yourself in one of those situations which are too difficult for a human being, when in judging, though innocent, one is guilty. There was once a Man who said: "Father, forgive them, for they know not what they do."

Kurt von Schuschnigg

The Sunflower in these latitudes is a symbol of autumn and not usually to be found on tombstones. What were the people thinking about who planted sunflowers in the military cemeteries of the Eastern Frontier or in the gardens laid out to conceal the unutterable misery that haunted the countless concentration camps? Those of all places, where mass murder was planned merely to safeguard the murderers' own security, a security which in fact was threatened by nobody.

"Madness" had become a "method" as incomprehensible for any rational being as it was in Hamlet's time. Today it seems as incredible to us as much else that happened at Lemberg and other places.

Psychological arguments and historically based pleas are a

waste of time—there is no possible justification for absolute evil, no matter when or by whom it is committed. But there is one explanation—the outburst of the animal element in man, the degradation of *Homo sapiens* to a mere machine. The herd immorality which in Nietzsche's words is "beyond good and evil".

Should one in the last resort forgive? No. On the contrary—for the simple reason that the whole business might very easily repeat itself. And not only amongst us Germans. Perhaps in any country where men have been "liberated" from all religious beliefs and thereby from all restraints.

Machiavelli, Hobbes, Spinoza, Nietzsche are quoted by theoreticians of a school of political science to which the idea of political ethics is quite unreal, but such quotations are unjustified, for the philosophers in question were thinking of power and what was feasible within the circumstances of their period. The opinion of Spinoza (*Tractatus Politicus*) that "everyone has as much right as he has power" had quite a different meaning in the 17th century from its meaning in the 20th.

This raises an objection, not to progress in technical matters, but to a distortion that often accompanies such progress.

For all progress must remain humanist, and man must never become a computer. This one must never, in heaven's name, forget, just because it is personally convenient to do so. Quite apart from the fact that there is in this problem no question of duty but rather (at least for those directly affected) of capability.

But just as one must not forget, there are also narrow limits imposed on forgiveness. One thing is certain: ideas of hatred and revenge are fruitless, like all chain reactions, for the reason that they are generalised emotions punishing both guilty and innocent indiscriminately. Punishment of the guilty is necessary as a deterrent. Many, even the majority of those who lay under the sunflowers, would not have wished otherwise. Countless destroyed or damaged lives, whole nations indeed, are, in juridical language, involved in a great historical process of punishment.

In *The Sunflower* story, the young mortally wounded SS man from Stuttgart was by no means basically evil, for he had a conscience. Nevertheless, he had been implicated in an atrocity which was outside the laws of war. Clearly he was not one of those who, from character or education or both, indulged in sadism and pleasure in torture for torture's sake. He was not one of those who in their youthful years had been wholly perverted by the materialism of the nonsensical "masterman" theory.

Years of SS training, however, corrupted him to such an extent that probably he simply obeyed orders, carried away by a blood lust that had nothing to do with war or soldiering. As a result, he acted in a way that no decent soldier, no matter in what situation he found himself, was entitled to act. If there was no chance of absenting himself, he could at least have fired in the air or he could have found difficulty in loading his rifle. Somehow or other he ought to have abstained from the crime.

Granted all this, nevertheless he was not a typical SS man. Soon the atrocious event had become for him an experience that persecuted and tortured his soul, an experience from which he could not escape. Until finally in the death chamber of the emergency hospital, the fear of death and eternal punishment, and the realisation of his wickedness, seized his conscience in an inexorable final grip. Gradually he had become again a decent human being and he strove for redemption.

The dream of "mastermen", among whom he might well have hoped to count himself, inevitably fades as life fades away. All at once it becomes horribly clear that instead of a masterman one is in fact a beast of prey. One longs to rejoin the human race. If nothing more is possible, at least to die like a human being. Thus it is not unreasonable, and not merely in a dying delirium, as at first seemed to be the case, that the former masterman should *in extremis* desire the moral support of a brother degraded to sub-humanity, so that he could at least end his botched life as a man.

Thus, according to *The Sunflower* story, there occurred the macabre meeting of the two helpless representatives of different worlds. The one on his deathbed who must talk because his conscience tormented him and felt himself already in hell. The other only an hour away from the inferno to which he has already half accustomed himself, so far as that was possible. He must listen, but he cannot speak. The dying man longs for a word of forgiveness: only a Jew, he feels, could raise him from the depths. The resulting encounter brought about by a silent nurse was improbable, secret, and presumably not free from danger. The Jewish visitor, robbed of freedom and human dignity, is faced by the question whether, after conscientiously considering every detail in the case, he could do what the dying man asked of him—forgive him.

A tragic problem—if indeed there was a problem at all. Anybody who tries to solve it will base his decision on how he himself would have acted in a similar case. In actual fact, the present writer would probably never have had the courage to obey the nurse's cryptic summons. But if he had done so, he would presumably have taken the earliest opportunity of quitting the sickroom with a soothing gesture to the dying SS man, conscious of his own powerlessness and the hopeless nature of the request. If possible he would probably have tried to arrange for any available cleric to visit the dying man.

One thing was certain, he could not, he should not, forgive. And had he forgiven it would have been a completely meaningless and thoroughly dishonest action. One can only pardon an offence which has been directly inflicted upon oneself.

Interpreted in the widest sense, and from an exclusively egotistic point of view, that would include even the extermination of one's own family. No one can forgive what others have suffered. The Creator alone, and nobody else, can forgive blood guilt and inhuman conduct. Moreover, it is only religious absolution that gives real meaning to forgiveness.

Was it an inhuman action to listen to the story and then walk away without a word, thereby refusing a dying man's last request? Certainly not. But it was a humane action to grant a last wish of a dying man merely by being willing to listen. Allowing him to talk—in the Catholic view one would call it confession—gave him the mental relief that he demanded. After recounting his wicked deed, he would be mentally alert enough to realise that there was nothing more for him to expect. He had repented and found a witness of his repentance. And he must have felt that thereby help had been vouchsafed to him. There is no other explanation possible for the fact that he wanted a silent Jewish visitor—the last person whom he saw on earth—to have his earthly possessions.

When after his death the nurse tried to hand these possessions over to the Jew, the latter quite understandably refused to accept them. But he carried away with him the memory of this strange encounter, and he seems to be the only person after the war to talk to the dead man's mother about her son.

The Sunflower casts sombre, but in the last resort, reconciliatory shadows.

Léopold Sédar Senghor

I do not claim to have lived the life of the Jewish martyrs in the concentration camps during the last world war. But I was almost shot to death after having been taken as a prisoner of war. So I at least know what it is to feel death only a quarter of an hour away.

I belonged to the French Resistance and there were nights when in my flat in Paris I expected to be arrested at any moment. Prior to this I had spent several months in an internment camp.

But I fully acknowledge that this is nothing compared with the suffering borne by millions of Jews in concentration camps during the second world war. The fact remains, however, that I am a Negro and that over a period of three hundred years twenty million negroes were deported to the United States of America whilst two hundred million were dying in Africa in the slave hunts.

I can understand your refusal to forgive. This is entirely in accordance with the spirit of the Bible, with the spirit of the Old Law. But there is the New Law, that of Christ as expressed in the Gospels. As a Christian, I think you should have forgiven.

I can recall that as we few dozen black soldiers stood before the firing squad on 20th June 1940 at La Charité-sur-Loire, I bore no hatred towards the SS men facing us. Needless to say it did not enter my head to forgive them since they had not asked me and since I was concerned, we were all chiefly concerned, with thinking of the cause, of the causes for which we were preparing to die: that is to say, the independence of France and the liberation of the black peoples.

Because I belong to an afflicted people, brother in suffering of the Jewish people, I can fully understand the suffering you underwent and also your unwillingness to forgive. But, once again, as a Christian and as a Negro, I would, I think, have forgiven the SS man. I stress: "I think". This does not mean to say that I would have done so. Perhaps, when it came to it, placed in the same circumstances as you, I would have acted as you did. I do not think I would have done but who knows?

How I, in Simon Wiesenthal's place, would have reacted to the request of the SS man, I cannot say. Perhaps I would have yielded from weakness, from a false kindness, and uttered the words of forgiveness for which the dying man longed. On the other hand, it may be that I would have acted in precisely the same way as Wiesenthal ... Yet it is true, leaving individual psychology out of consideration, that even in such a situation the individual acts in accordance with his character. As to the question of conscience placed before every reader of the epilogue to *The Sunflower*, one must first of all establish the following principle: it is possible for us to forget a wrong, even the worst misdeed which has been committed on us. If that happens, the question of forgiveness is superfluous. Why and through what internal process we are able to reach such a state of forgetting, cannot here be discussed. Apart from any forgetting which the victim is able to achieve, there is forgetting on the part of the evildoer, an incomparably more frequent phenomenon. Certainly there is a deep psychological feeling that there can be no final oblivion. In this case it is a question of a more or less lasting "disactualisation".

Must one forget before one can forgive? Is it possible to retain the misdeed in one's memory and nevertheless forgive it? What are the conditions in which such a thing can happen?

The first answer may sound cynical: the surest and most lasting forgiveness and reconciliation is when the descendants of the evildoers and those of the victims bind themselves into a collective and unbreakable unity—into a family, a tribe, a people, a nation. Ernest Renan, some hundred years ago, pointed out that the existence of nations depends on forgetting. Each nation represents the amalgamation of tribes who for many years, and possibly for hundreds of years, had inflicted the worst sufferings and griefs on each other. Each new generation discovers the truth about the frightful shattering past, but that does not destroy the consciousness of a common destiny.

A second tragic possibility—it comes nearer our case because of the one-sidedness of the crime—is that of extreme humiliation and ruthless persecution. In order not to have their lives fatally imperilled, the victims or their descendants subject themselves to their wrongdoers and admit that their lies and excuses are true. Whence the at least temporary success of the totalitarian oppressor and tyrant.

In both cases a purposeful "disactualisation" takes place, in order to free the present and more especially the future from the heavy burden of the past. Does the forgetting in that case precede the crime, or vice versa? In each case the answer may be different. True, the old Jewish principle frequently applies: kulo chajav—all are guilty. And so all are guilty, and all may go free. Punishment would be too awful, it would endanger the existence of mankind, and mankind must not perish.

Doubtless one could formulate the problem in another way: do the evildoers themselves forget, do they forget before they have repented and confessed their crime? Without confession and sincere repentance their forgetting is nothing more than a continuation of their crime. So do not grant pardon before you are certain that the guilty on their side will always remember their guilt. From this point of view the ethical problem facing both Jews and Germans is not a simple one, but it is completely clear—before we have the right to forget, we must be absolutely certain that the Germans on their side have not forgotten, and that they are willing to do everything possible so as not to forget the crimes committed in their name. The two peoples are bound together in startling fashion by the terrible events, just as the young SS man on his deathbed and the prisoner Wiesenthal were bound together. And Wiesenthal will be bound until his dying day. Though their misdeeds and their sufferings may make it enormously difficult to live together in lasting peace, yet nothing now can separate them from each other.

I always rejected, both in theory and practice, the idea of collective guilt, but I do believe that there is such a thing as national or State responsibility. In this respect the reparations made by the German Federal Republic to Israel and to the surviving victims of Nazi crimes are entirely justified and significant. They replace nothing, they cannot reverse what has happened, but for the Germans they are a psychohygienic necessity. But that is no answer to the question: how can one forgive those who make it impossible for us to forget—so far as we would dare to forget—because they on their side are determined to behave as though they no longer know what there is to forgive and forget?

If the young SS man was guilty, yet he differed from the organisers of the extermination camps and the accomplices of genocide. By his obedience to his criminal leaders he augmented the guilt which he had incurred by putting himself politically and unconditionally at their disposal. There is no question of that, but it is none less true that in the end he brought the accusation against himself. As an accused person he is condemned in our eyes and rejected, but as accuser he placed himself among the victims.

Nevertheless Simon Wiesenthal was quite right in refusing to pardon him, at any rate not in the name of the martyrs, who neither then nor now had entrusted anybody with such a mission. But if that young man had lived and remained true to the convictions which tortured the last hours of his life, and maybe even transfigured him—if he were still among us would Wiesenthal condemn him? I think not. And I feel that I too could not condemn that SS man today.

The corrupt autocrats forced upon their subjects a complicity from which only he could escape who followed the dictates of his conscience even when thereby he risked his life. Thus it was that millions of people were guilty. Let none of us refuse to forgive any one of them whose guilt became the irrepressible source of a tortured conscience. There can be no counter-argument against forgiveness in such a case, or indeed against a reconciliation based on pity.

Friedrich Torberg

I have read your book with great sympathy, with great emotion, and—as your work was known to me in advance—with great anxiety whether I would be able to offer even half-adequate comment, or indeed whether I ought to make any comment at all. On the whole I think not. A book of this nature must speak for itself—and I think that *The Sunflower* does this most admirably. It needs neither "recommendation" nor "evaluation". I am precluded by an almost invincible shyness when faced with books of this type—especially when (like yours) they are based on actual experience—from giving any "judgment". I can only assure you that I consider your book successful from a literary viewpoint also, that its effect is doubled by its sobriety, that its characters are as credible and vivid as the events portrayed. I speak from a professional writer's viewpoint. Of course I am more pleased to be able to say this than I should have been had I had to say the opposite, but I am still rather reluctant to say it.

Perhaps you are acquainted with my story "Mein ist die Rache" (Revenge is mine), which treats of a similarly insoluble problem. The question of the right to revenge, which is my theme, is just as difficult to answer as your question of the right to forgive. With a feeling of embarrassment closely related to yours, I believe one is justified in thinking that the point is not that such questions should be answered, but that they should be raised at all.

If today, after all your experiences you are still worried by the question whether you should have forgiven a Nazi murderer, that very fact is far more valid evidence of an intact morality than if you had actually forgiven him. It is in this intact morality—I should like to hope, and I give it as a parting present to your book—that we are superior to the others, to the murderers and to those who held their peace about the murders when they were committed and are still holding their peace today.

Contributors

RENÉ CASSIN (1887–) is a distinguished French jurist, former president and member (1946–68) of the Human Rights Commission of the United Nations, and principal author of its *Universal Declaration of the Rights of Man.* He was awarded the Nobel Peace Prize in 1968 and is the recipient of many French awards, including Officier de la Résistance (1945) and the Grand Croix de la Légion d'Honneur (1958).

DAVID DAICHES (1912–), the eminent British university professor, has taught at Balliol College, Oxford; Cambridge University; University of Sussex; University of Chicago; and Cornell University. A noted literary critic, he is the author of some thirty-five books, including the two-volume *Critical History of English Literature* and the recent *Moses: The Man and His Vision.* He is the recipient of many literary awards and prizes.

CONSTANTINE FITZGIBBON (1919–) is an Irish author and translator. His works include *Denazification* and *A Concise History of Germany,* as well as the translation of Manès Sperber's *The Achilles Heel.*

EDWARD H. FLANNERY is a member of the National Conference of Catholic Bishops' Secretariat for Catholic-Jewish Relations. Father Flannery is also author of *The Anguish of the Jews,* the preface of which was written by Monsignor John M. Oesterreicher, a contributor to this Symposium.

HERBERT GOLD (1924–) is a noted American author who has taught at Cornell University, University of California at Berkeley, Harvard, Stanford, and University of California at Davis. He is the author of *Birth of a Hero, The Man Who Was Not With It, The Prospect Before Us, The Optimist, Love and Like, Therefore Be Bold, Salt,* and *Fathers.*

MARK GOULDEN is a British journalist and publisher. He began his career as reporter and editor for several newspapers and periodicals and is now chairman of W. H. Allen and Co., Publishers, in London. He is an activist in humanitarian causes and has received innumerable citations and awards.

HANS HABE (1911–) was born in Hungary and educated in Vienna and Heidelberg. His auspicious literary career began as a reporter and newspaper editor in Vienna, followed by an assignment to the League of Nations as correspondent for a Geneva newspaper. His most noted book, *The Mission,* is a documentary novel on the Evian Conference in 1938, which sought to deal with the refugee problem resulting from Nazi persecutions. After World War II, he was editor-in-chief of *Die Neue Zeitung* (Munich). A recipient of the Herzl Prize, his most recent works include *Poisoned Stream* and *Proud Zion.*

FRIEDRICH HEER (1916–) was born in Vienna and is professor of cultural history at the University of Vienna. The author of numerous essays on historical subjects, he is also well known as chief dramatist at the Burgtheater in Vienna.

GUSTAV W. HEINEMANN (1899–) was president of the Federal Republic of Germany from 1969 to 1974. A noted jurist and politician, he has also served as federal minister of the interior and of justice following World War II.

ABRAHAM J. HESCHEL (1907–1972) was a noted theologian and educator. Born in Warsaw, he taught extensively in Europe before coming to the United States in 1940. He taught Jewish philosophy, ethics, and mysticism, primarily at the Jewish Theological Seminary of America and was the author of numerous books, most notably *Between God and Man: An Interpretation of Judaism, The Insecurity of Freedom: Essays in Human Existence,* and *Man Is Not Alone: A Philosophy of Religion.*

CHRISTOPHER HOLLIS (1902–) is a noted British journalist and author, also a former member of Parliament. He served in the R.A.F. during World War II and is the author of many books including *Church and Economics, The Papacy,* and *Holy Places: Jewish, Christian and Muslim Monuments in the Holy Land.*

ROGER IKOR, the distinguished French author, has received the Prix Goncourt as well as many other awards for his literary achievements and humanitarian efforts in opposition to racialism.

JACOB KAPLAN (1895–) has served as chief rabbi of France since 1955. He is a member of l'Institut Académique des Sciences Morales et Politiques and author of several books on Judaism, particularly French Jewry, including *Le Judaism et la Justice Sociale, French Jewry under the Occupation* and *Le Judaisme dans la Société Contemporaine.* The recipient of many honors, including the Médaille d'Honneur des Oeuvres Sociales, Rabbi Kaplan is a Commandeur de la Légion d'Honneur.

ROBERT M. W. KEMPNER (1899–), jurist of international renown, was born in Germany and educated at the universities of Berlin, Breslau, and Freiburg. Forced to flee Nazi Germany he taught in Florence and Nice, before coming to the United States, where he became counselor to President Roosevelt. He served as U. S. prosecutor on Justice Robert Jackson's staff at the Nuremberg Trials. A contributor to many professional journals, Kempner's literary works include *Twilight of Justice, Eichmann and Accomplices, SS Under Cross-examinations,* and *Edith Stein and Anne Frank—Two of a Hundred Thousand.*

HERMANN KESTEN (1900–) is an American writer, born in Germany and educated there and in Italy. He has lived in the United States since 1940 and is the author and editor of some forty books including *Der Gerechte, Guernika, The Twins of Nuremberg, Emile Zola,* and *Heart of Europe.* He is the recipient of the Kleist Prize and the City of Nuremberg literary prize.

MILTON R. KONVITZ (1908–) was born in Safed, Israel, and came to the United States as a child in 1915. He practiced law for several years; served as assistant general counsel for the NAACP (1943–46); and taught at New York University, The New School for Social Research, and Cornell University. He is now professor emeritus of industrial relations and labor relations, and of law at Cornell. His works include *Judaism and Human Rights* and *Religious Liberty and Conscience.*

PRIMO LEVI (1919–) is an Italian executive and author who was graduated from the University of Turin in 1941. In 1943 he was arrested by the Italian Fascisti, and in 1944 transferred from an Italian detention camp to Auschwitz, where he remained until the camp was liberated in 1945. He described his ordeal in Auschwitz camp in his book, *If This Is a Man,* and tells of his long return journey to Italy via the Soviet Union in a sequel volume, *The Reawakening.*

POUL GEORG LINDHARDT (1910–) is a Danish minister and professor of religion, and is past dean of the faculty of divinity at Aarhus University. He is also the author of numerous books on religion.

SALVADOR DE MADARIAGA (1886–), the Spanish diplomat and writer, served as Spanish ambassador in Washington and in Paris, and was primary Spanish delegate to the League of Nations (1931–36). He is the author of many books including *Genius of Spain, Morning Without Noon, Portrait of Europe, Spain: A Modern History, The Price of Peace, Anarchy or Hierarchy,* and *The World's Design.*

GABRIEL MARCEL (1889–1973) was an eminent French philosopher and writer. He taught for many years and worked in collaboration with the publishing houses of Plon and Grasset. He was awarded the Frankfurt Peace Prize in 1964, and his literary output included *Existential Background of Human Dignity, Man Against Mass Society,* and the two-volume *The Mystery of Being.*

HERBERT MARCUSE (1898–) left his native Germany in 1934 to teach philosophy at Columbia University, and subsequently at Harvard University, Brandeis University, and the University of California at San Diego. During World War II he served with the U.S. Office of Strategic Services and the State Department (1941–50). He is the author of numerous books including *Eros and Civilization, One-Dimensional Man, Counter-Revolution and Revolt,* and *Studies in Critical Philosophy.*

JACQUES MARITAIN (1882–1973) was an eminent French philosopher and professor at Princeton and Columbia universities as well as several European universities. He was the author of many works, including *A Christian Looks at the Jewish Question, Christianity and Democracy,* and *Integral Humanism.*

MARTIN E. MARTY (1928–) is a well-known American theologian, editor, and educator. He has taught at numerous colleges and universities and at present is professor of modern church history at the Divinity School of the University of Chicago. He is the author of *The Fire We Can Light: The Role of Religion in a Suddenly Different World, Hidden Discipline, Protestantism,* and *Short History of Christianity,* among others.

JOHN M. OESTERREICHER, who is director of the Institute of Judaeo-Christian Studies at Seton Hall University and of its graduate program, narrowly escaped arrest by the Gestapo, first in Vienna, in 1938, and later in Paris, in 1940. As consultor at Vatican II, he wrote the statement of principles that led to the Council's declaration on the Church's bond to the Jewish people.

CYNTHIA OZICK is the author of a novel, *Trust;* a collection of short stories, *The Pagan Rabbi;* a novella, *An Education,* and the recently published collection of short works, *Bloodshed. And Three Novellas.* She has published numerous essays, reviews, literary criticism, and translations as well, and has been nominee and recipient of many literary awards, including a National Book Award nomination in 1972.

JAMES WILLIAM PARKES (1896–) is a British theologian and historian who has written extensively on Judaism and Judeao-Christian relations. His Parkes Library, now housed at Southampton University, is a distinguished collection of books and documents on Jewish-Christian relations. Among his own works are *Antisemitism, Judaism and Christianity, Conflict of the Church and the Synagogue: A Study in the Origins of Antisemitism,* and *Prelude to Dialogue: Jewish-Christian Relationships.*

TERENCE PRITTIE (1913–), the noted British journalist and author, reported from West Germany for the *Manchester Guardian* from 1946 to 1963. Since leaving the *Guardian* in 1970, he has served as a political consultant on Middle East affairs for the BBC and other news agencies. He is the author of *Germans Against Hitler, Adenauer: Portrait of a Statesman,* and *Willy Brandt: Portrait of a Statesman,* among several other works.

LUISE RINSER (1911–) is a well-known German author and specialist in psychology. A schoolteacher before World War II, she was imprisoned by the Nazis. After the war she became literary critic of *Die Neue Zeitung* (Munich). She is married to the noted German composer Carl Orff.

KURT VON SCHUSCHNIGG (1897–) is an Austrian statesman and professor of political science. He served as minister of justice in the Buresch and Dollfuss cabinets, and became federal chancellor after Dollfuss' assassination in 1934. He served in various ministerial posts from 1936 until the Nazi Putsch in March 1938, when he was arrested. He was liberated by the Allied troops in May 1945. From 1948 to 1968, he was professor of political science at Saint Louis University in Missouri.

LÉOPOLD SÉDOR SENGHOR (1906–), the Senegalese politician and writer, was a deputy of Senegal to the French National Assembly from 1946 to 1958, and later was president of the Federal Assembly, Mali Federation of Senegal and Sudan. He was recipient of the Dag Hammarskjöld Prize in 1965.

MANÈS SPERBER (1905–), French author and editor, was born in Galicia and spent his youth in Vienna where he studied psychology with Alfred Adler. He subsequently taught in Berlin and escaped to France when the Nazis came to power. He joined the publishing house of Calmann-Levy, and turned to literature, first writing in German, then in French. Among his best-known works are *The Burned Bramble, The Abyss, Journey Without End, The Achilles Heel,* and *Man and His Deeds.*

FRIEDRICH TORBERG (1908–) is an Austrian author and editor. He won fame early in his career with the novel *Der Schuler Gerber hat absolviert.* Forced to flee from the Nazis in 1938, he joined a Czech brigade of the French army, and in 1940 came to the United States. The fate of the Jews under the Nazis forms the theme of his novella, *Mein ist die Rache,* and of his novel, *Hier bin ich, mein Vater.* After his return to Vienna in 1951, he edited the literary monthly, *Forum.* Among his most recent publications are *Der ewige Refrain, Das fünfte Rad am Thespiskarren,* and *Golems Wiederkehr.*